God Hates Religion

Some Day He will do away with them all

James M Raines

All scripture quotations, unless otherwise indicated, are taken from the New King James Version ®. Copyright © 1982 by Thomas Nelson, Inc. Used by permission. All rights reserved.

Taken from the Complete Jewish Bible by David H. Stern. Copyright © 1998. All rights reserved. Used by permission of Messianic Jewish Publishers, 6120 Day Long Lane, Clarksville, MD 21029. www.messianicjewish.net.

Excerpt taken from the Five Books of Moses, authored by C. Everett Fox and by permission of Schocken Books, Inc. a division of Random House, Inc.

ISBN: 978-0-615-99712-4

Copyright © 2012 by James M Raines.

2014 edition © revised and updated by James M Raines

All rights reserved, including the right of reproduction in whole or in part in any form, world wide.

Acknowledgments

I am thankful for my Christian motorcycling buddies Colin Harley Ott (yep, his actual middle name) and Donald "Ozie" Osburn. I shared with Oz this search for the ancient path to the Almighty. He was interested in my findings, but unsure how to apply them. For years we did not give up on each other. When the pathway to the Almighty emerged, he was conflicted and he stopped next to the trail one foot on, one foot off:

May Yehovah bless Colin and Ozie and keep them; Cause Your Face to shine upon them and be gracious to them. May Yehovah lift up your Countenance upon Colin and Ozie and give them peace.

My thanks to Claire Eyton, for her proofreading generosity.

I'm a lifelong fan of Dr. J. Vernon McGee, whose radio broadcasts blessed me during my car traveling work years and his influence continues to this day. His occasional criticism of Christianity for failing to connect with Israel is in a special place in my mind and helped set in motion this Hebraic search for Yehovah's ancient Ways.

I am very appreciative of the original work of these Torah minded Hebrew scholars, experts in their fields. I was fortunate to discover their excellent knowledge. These are my Hebrew experts in the order I found them: Sid Roth, Jonathon Bernis, Michael Rood, David Stern, Nehemiah Gordon, Simca Jacobovici, Gabriel Barkay, James D. Tabor, Orly Goldwasser and Geza Vermes.

My wife Connie enjoyed my search for the trail to the Creator and the excitement as good finds were shared with her. At first she was reluctant to leave the social life and music of our church. When the beautiful pathway to the Almighty emerged, that all changed and we returned together to the Way of her ancestors.

Many daughters of Israel have lived courageously, but you surpass them all.

CONTENTS

Preface	7
Introduction	8
Prologue	24
Chapter 1. God Gave Speeches to the Hebrews?	25
Chapter 2. The Hebrews Still Face Us	28
Chapter 3. The Pagan Roots of Christianity	36
Chapter 4. Princes of This World	57
Chapter 5. The Name God Calls Himself	61
Chapter 6. Torah Has No Peer. Even Classical Greek Thinkers Astounded	65
Chapter 7. Semitic Sources of NT scriptures	74
Chapter 8. Sayings of Adonai Dishonored	78
Chapter 9. The Christian NT	90
Chapter 10. Glossary of Semitic Words	93
Chapter 11. Yehovah's Torah Way of Life	120
Chapter 12. Co Stars of the NT	125
Summary	137
Appendix	148
Bibliography	152

Preface

I didn't write this book because I feel that my religious experiences are unusual. I wrote this book because I have heard ✝ teachings for 60 years that do not follow God's Teachings in the bible. In the first example of many, God condemned *public displays* of religious behavior (prayer, fasting, mourning, giving alms) in His ancient teachings more than a thousand years before Jesus' time. In Matthew 6, 1 to 18 Jesus' teachings to his followers repeated God's public display condemnations. Yet, praying in front of others is encouraged and even integral to the operation of modern Christian churches! The fact is that the Almighty just does not like human audiences when someone is sacrificing for Him or speaking to Him in order to be **seen by men.** How are we to deal with this disrespect for Yehovah's words? Here's what I have done: There is a verse that says 'Train up a child in the *way* he should go and when he is old he will not depart from it'. Well, Christianity departed from the *way* of its Torah roots and consequently I've departed from church.

Both departures because the church's *way* is not the Way described in the bible. Jesus himself opined this of certain rootless people (Sadducees) in his day: **You err, not knowing the scriptures** *(Matt.22, 29)*. Since the New Testament (NT) had not been written yet, Jesus could only be referring to Hebrew Torah Scriptures also called the Old Testament (OT). The first five books, Torah *proper*, are the ancient history of the nation of Israel's experiences of God's Presence dwelling on their land. But in English bible translations even the name of the roots, the word Torah itself was replaced by the vague Latin derived term *scriptures*. Modern English bible translations show no regard for the ancient biblical words in their context, thus ancient Ways of Yehovah (the *way*) is not taught to believers in churches.

This revised 2014 edition of **God Hates Religion** (GHR) takes into account newly found information about the significance of key Semitic words in the bible. Jesus' quotes of Torah do connect the NT directly to Torah. This book describes the original meanings of a number of these Torah words in their Hebrew sociolinguistic context at their time of writing up to 1500 years before Jesus. The new part is gleaned from Geza Vermes: Individual believers now have a way to be *both* follower of Jesus and observer of Yehovah's Torah Ways. GHR contains 9 years of my literature research on this subject and 30 years of challenges establishing Yehovah's Words in my life. I hope this book will be a lifelong blessing for you.

   May 14, 2011, Revised July 15, 2014

   James M Raines

   Fortuna, California, USA

Introduction [1]

In the English versions of the NT record Jesus quotes only Torah passages as the sole authority for his teachings. He relied totally on the ancient Hebrew Words in his Father's Torah. As the ancient rabbis of his time found out, Jesus intimately understood the Words in his Father's Torah and from a very early age (Luke 2, 41 to 50). It is evident in the manner in which he conducted himself that as early as age 12 Yeshua personified His Father's Ways. He was Torah in the flesh. The rabbis were amazed at this. Torah became how he lived, his doctrine. We try to do the same. And there is little faith required to incorporate his teachings and personal examples, IF one possesses knowledge of Torah. While the English NT has an overall theme of faith in the Gospel running through it, Jesus' Torah uses the theme *trust*, a term emphasizing the power of Yehovah's Words to define His Character, His Ways. Since Jesus only cites Torah as his standard of truth, we must also! Any teaching in the NT writings not found in Torah is a human addition breaking from Yehovah's original teaching in Paleo Hebrew. The new theme of *faith* is an obvious example of an un***author***ized (not from Yehovah) change to Torah.

You will read in this book some bold statements intended to prepare you to discover the oldest yet most discredited knowledge of the Almighty. An ancient Middle Eastern people began to enjoy it some four thousand years ago. This would be a daunting proposition for you. What you have here, in the short timeline of reading a relatively small book, took this researcher about 30 years of adjustments and transformations in tiny steps to find and honor Yehovah's Words. There is no way to present the features of this story to you all at once. It will be valuable for you to place your natural skepticism on hold while reading this book. I hope you will accept these first statements at face value for a time with the joy of seeking Yehovah's Ways. Very few of these are my ideas, just relaying them to you. While it may all be unfamiliar to you, there is little new knowledge here. You have here few propositions newer than two to four thousand years; And those only for your convenience and because they speak to the ancient ways. Many claims may not at first make sense to you. Try looking for key words in the glossary chapter. Parts of

---

[1] *To find out how this book came about, read Appendix 1, sometime later.*

this book may have to be read multiple times, or in the future before the picture comes together. And please realize descriptions of the factual shortcomings of religion are meant only to free our minds to know and understand Yehovah's plans, His Ways and so to know and understand Yehovah.

We routinely credit Jesus with new teachings: [Love your neighbor as yourself.] Matthew 22, 39. However millennia before Jesus' times, his Father Yehovah said, [but you shall love your neighbor as yourself] Leviticus (the heart of Torah) 19, 18b. Neighborly love is an ancient Way of Yehovah that is given to us as a statute. The fullness of God's thinking resides in the Torah contexts of various NT accounts of Jesus' personal life. The complete statutory thought of Yehovah is found in Leviticus 19, in the surrounding verses 17 through 19: *[Verse 17. You shall not hate your brother in your heart. You shall surely rebuke your neighbor, and not bear sin because of him. 18. You shall not take vengeance, nor bear any grudge against the children of your people, but you shall love your neighbor as yourself. I am Yehovah. 19. You shall keep My statutes]*. Note that in all these personal actions, the standard is the keeping of Torah: *You shall keep My statutes*. If one does not know His Torah, one cannot "keep" or live by His statutes. If one *does* know the Torah context of Jesus' teachings, the fullness of Yehovah's Ways is revealed in concrete terms. How much theoretical *faith* then is required to live by them? None, only *trust* in Yehovah and the authenticity of His Words. The true follower of Yeshua, who desires to be "sold out for the Lord", must go down the same pathway. For the *enabled* follower of Yeshua, the error of not knowing Scriptures vanishes.

Jesus didn't just make up his teachings out of thin air, he incorporated them into his life by personally following his father's Ways from written Torah as it was read to him. In the second half of the first century, at different times in various places, new traditions filled in and Jesus' Torah teachings were replaced as gentile christians separated themselves from anything Hebrew. Hundreds of years later all this was codified into civil and religious law by the Roman Emperor Constantine. Without a single conversion, people of all faiths throughout Constantine's Empire became "Christians" overnight. Any Hebrew or Jewish religious thing became illegal. All writings in Hebrew were destroyed. Constantine excised all Hebrew *roots* from "Christian" beliefs and introduced pagan foreign worship traditions which gradually became traditional Christian beliefs. These new traditions gained a false validity over the next 1700 years. Today modern believers concentrate on English NT texts where Jesus only briefly reiterates an issue in Yehovah's Torah. We are cut off by traditions resistant to the rich context of Yehovah's Torah. So now, it is *we* who err.

A believer seeking to know and understand the Father's Thinking through Jesus' teachings is actually going about it backwards. This book points out that Jesus' teachings are in fact later living commentary on his Father's original Torah Words. Jesus' teachings direct our attention to the earlier authority of Torah. Over the centuries various Church teachings have come and gone while Torah has not changed. It remains the Bedrock of Yehovah's Plans for human beings. Advanced imaging technology recently applied to surviving ancient Torah copies demonstrates Torah in use today is the same as Torah dated 2000+ years of age. Jesus' use of that Torah some 2000 years ago as the authority for his teachings strongly implies Torah of today has fidelity extending back another 1300 to 1500 years to the ancient author Moses' signature writing of Torah!

This book's title *God Hates Religion* has an element of shock value but is meant to start a certain clashing of thoughts in your mind. You may recall the mental juggling when you first saw it: Isn't religion the route to God? Why would God hate that? (Answer: He hates changes to His Words.) The terms God, Almighty, Father, El, Yahweh and Yehovah will refer to the Creator of the universe: the God of Adam, Noah, Abraham, Moses, the biblical Prophets, Jesus and many, many others.

Here's our situation: Western religions, the Christian faiths, all have a common historical origin. It is Torah, Moses' written documentation of both the Almighty's speeches to Israel 3500 years ago and His ensuing talks with Moses over the next 40+ years (Exodus 24, 1 to 4). **Virtually all modern western religions have separated themselves from Torah.** In America, the bible standard for Christians has over the last few centuries become what is written in the English New Testament. From the beginning of Jesus' ministry it was not so. Whereas the people of Israel agreed 3500 years ago to follow all God's Instructions relayed to them via Moses, virtually all western religions have reversed this by *adapting* Yehovah's Torah teachings to western foreign culture. This is backwards. This minimizing of Torah's effect on NT teachings effectively forces us into following Constantine's paganized version of Jesus' teachings. Torah is made of no effect, to use the language of Matt.15, 6b. This prophetically fulfills what Jesus envisioned in his indictment, *You err, not knowing Torah.* Over time these western adaptations morphed into creative *replacements* breaking from the original thinking Yehovah expressed [2] in Torah. Torah is where the oldest documented events of the bible and His original teachings for Israel and mankind are located. The Almighty anticipated human creativity's work on His Words and told Moses to write this caution: ***Do not change My Words*** (Deut. 4, 2). To the extent English NT changes Torah, we are all

---

[2] *Deuteronomy 4, 2 to 4; Jeremiah 6, 19.*

at risk. Claiming the ideas of men are equal to the higher thoughts of the Creator cannot be reality: Isaiah 55, 8 to 13; Jeremiah 6, 10b and 20.

The Creator's original Torah teachings are most important for humans to experience because they reveal His ancient Ways in His own Words. If we change His Words, we will not know His Ways, how then will we understand Him and follow His Ways? Knowing and understanding Yehovah is the essence of the Plan for human life on earth (read it in Jeremiah 9, 22 and 23). In the last half of my life as a Christian I became aware of a number of *replaced* Ways of Yehovah. The first sign of all this appeared about 30 years ago. In Matthew 6, 1 to 18 Jesus is reported to have told his followers not to give to the poor, fast, nor **pray** in the presence of other people. These were not new commandments but reiterations of individual teachings in Torah, torahs. In Matthew 6, 6 the torah is to pray *only* in privacy. Yet the Christian world massively ignores this reiterated torah from Jesus. In later years, as discrepancies like this piled up I participated less and less enthusiastically in my ancestral religion. Shortly after the turn of the 21st century I sought to resolve all this for myself. Setting out with equal *faith* in both Old and New Testament accounts I decided to find out once and for all what it truly is that God has said. I vowed to find out what is on God's Mind *no matter what*. Eventually *it came to me* to search for the original Hebrew meanings of the bible's words via ancient Hebrew biblical commentary nowadays available in English by Hebrew biblical experts. A year or so into this process *it came to me* to spend my time reading commentary on ancient Hebrew Scriptures only from experts reared in Hebrew culture who are native speakers of Hebrew. For reasons that will be explained later in this book, this is the only genuine opportunity these days to understand the original meanings of Torah's ancient Hebrew words. It became clear that the work of gentile commentators all consisted of retreads of the many old circular explanations I'd tired of in fifty+ years of church. It's how they all roll. Their explanations did not lead to the desired advance toward the Hebrew roots of the bible, but rather circled back to their own notions of what is holy; Ideas from theology, the western foreigner's Torah deficient academic study of God. If a teaching is not to be found in Torah (Mind of God) it's from the mind of a human.

It is news to no one that Christians and Hebrews are far apart in their respective opinions of Yahweh's Torah. Specifically, Torah observant Jews and a few gentiles view Torah as the only document worthy of guiding one's personal life in the modern world. Christian theologies however view Torah as a total burden, impossible to achieve and irrelevant to modern life since it has been replaced by their English scriptures and derivatively by their traditions. They are separated from Torah. The Ancient of Days, the Living God of Israel has His own opinion: **"For**

this mitzvah [Torah] **which I am giving you today is not too hard for you, it is not beyond your reach."** [3] Churches overestimate their traditions and dismiss this clear message from Yehovah that Torah is not too hard for people to know and live out.

This book intends to challenge western religious mentalities and add depth to the individual believer's relationship with Yehovah, but not convert anyone to or from any religion. Let us use the Almighty's point of view to examine the message He told us about Himself in His Speeches to Israel 3500 years ago. Below you will find evidence demonstrating that Jesus exhibited that same goal: to teach the Ways of Yehovah found in Torah. In fact, Jesus states he is inseparable from Torah. But first consider that Yehovah's own words tell us what's on Yehovah's Mind; He wants human beings to *understand* and *know* Him.

"Thus says [Yehovah]: Let not the wise man glory in his wisdom, Let not the mighty man glory in his might, Nor let the rich man glory in his riches; But let him who glories glory in this, That he understands and knows Me, That I am [Yehovah], exercising loving kindness, judgment, and righteousness in the earth. For in these I delight," says [Yehovah]. Jeremiah 9, 23, 24.

Greek thinkers and western theologians are examples of wise men who do not practice, understand nor value Torah knowledge of Yehovah. In contrast, in Matthew 5, 17 to 19 Jesus defends ancient Torah and glues himself to Torah with this:

☛ **"Do not think that I came to destroy the Law [Torah] or the Prophets. I did not come to destroy but to fulfill** (both Torah and Prophets!). **For assuredly, I say to you, till heaven and earth pass away, one jot or one tittle will by no means pass from Torah till all is fulfilled. Whoever therefore breaks one of the least of these [torahs] and teaches men so, shall be called least in the kingdom of heaven; but whoever does and teaches them, he shall be called great in the kingdom of heaven."**

The word *destroy* means change in that it destroys meaning. *Fulfill* means fill full. On the basis of these words of Jesus, the NT cannot theologically replace Torah, the path to the ancient Ways of Yehovah. **Torah IS the "Way" spoken of in the NT.** Jesus *represented* the "Way" in the flesh. When he says, "I am the way", he is saying "I, Torah in the flesh, am the Way." "I am the way" is not a new teaching. Jesus had no new teachings. He lived for Israel to return to Torah, the ancient Ways of God. But, return from what? In Jesus' times it was *from* the teachings of the ancient rabbis who claimed Moses gave them a second, unwritten Torah, an oral Torah which only they could interpret. Nowadays it would be *from* western theological translations which produced a changed NT, as it were, a New Torah.

---

[3]*Deuteronomy 30,11: Complete Jewish Bible. And understand it by reading the whole section.*

Final point: there is a story in Matthew 15, 24 where Jesus turns down a Samaritan (gentile) woman's help request for her daughter. Yeshua explained: *"...I have come only for the lost house of Israel..."*, meaning he had come only to return the ten northern tribes to written Torah of Moshe. This is a wake up call for all NT believers, whose churches don't teach Jesus' message: **I did not come for gentiles**.

Yehovah anticipated human changes to His Words. In Deuteronomy 4, 2 the Almighty says:

"You shall not add to the word [Torah] which I command you, nor take from it, that you may keep the commandments [Ways] of the Lord your God which I command [teach] you."

By implication, Torah is complete and will never need change. Here's the sobering FACT, predating earth's creation which explains to us the Almighty's caution against changing His words:

"For My thoughts [plans] are not your thoughts, Nor are your ways My ways....For as the heavens are higher than the earth, So are My ways higher than your ways, And My thought than your thoughts..... Isaiah 55, 8 to13. Yehovah goes on to say that He makes rain and snow fall to the earth where it remains in order to provide food for his all His earthly creatures, as do His Words. So, theology, the western foreigner's Torah deficient academics are not God's Ways.

For interpretation of biblical terms in this book you will find a Hebrew biblical perspective of Yehovah's Words. It is a composite gleaned from the expert Hebrew Torah Keepers identified in this books's acknowledgments and bibliography sections. I'm no Torah expert, but they are. So, what good are the thoughts of this ignorant English speaking gentile? My function, in addition to finding and passing Hebrew expert perspective to you, is to point out the many steps needed to adapt the teachings of my inherited Christian religion to the ancient Ways of Yehovah: keeping it chronological. This experience is probably not available from Hebrew experts. The purpose of providing you with descriptions of these steps is to familiarize you with Yehovah's Ways as the alternative to your churches' teachings. After all, no one believes everything taught by their church which is in a continual state of change anyway. Our dilemma as believers is to consider ourselves in Yehovah's Presence yet continuing to live the lies from the Roman Emperor Constantine's foreign paganizing of Jesus' teachings. Many examples are found throughout rest of this book and are especially available in the Glossary.

God did not choose English to document His Torah speeches, He chose two of the Semitic languages, Hebrew and Aramaic. Let us all consider Torah in the socieolinguistic contexts that came with the languages the Almighty did choose. He did not choose Rome nor the USA, but Jerusalem and *eretz Israel*; Not Greeks but Hebrews, Jews. God's Words caution us not to follow any substituted words which destroy the significance of His ancient Thoughts. Otherwise no one will know how to live life by Yehovah's Ways and we will not duplicate our Master, Yeshua. As more believers observe Torah the 43,800 denominations should whittle themselves down. It was never Jesus' intent for his teachings to spawn 43,800 divisions, he claimed perfect unity in his unity prayer. This book advocates Yehovah's Torah as unity glue and the preexisting Plan to which today's western religious traditions are all defocused alternatives.

Recently the number of religions existing worldwide has been numbered at just over ten thousand.[4] Christianity itself is catalogued at 34,800 sects, movements or denominations! Each of these 34,800 is distinct each believes that their understanding of the Almighty is right and other's are not. Many also function as the secular structure of everyday society in their respective geographical areas. They infuse religious expectations into their social structure (see Marriage, ch. 10). Historically that has been true of America, but the times are changing. Isaiah 55, 8 says the Almighty's unique plan for humanity is far above the din of thousands of cultures of religious experience worldwide. What if the Almighty were to design His own human culture from the ground up and start it in a Way that enabled its longevity and fidelity to His ancient Plans for earth? How would it be if a new nation of peoples were rounded up, instructed in the Almighty's divine cultural practices, given their own land upon which to work all this out and given a mission for all earth's people? That scenario describes Torah and the nation of Israel.

Christianity's 34,800+ movements world wide is what we HAVE. What we WANT is God's identity in a small elegant package, the **E=MC**^{2} for God. Well, we do have it. God revealed His Identity and plans for earth to Moses 3500 years ago. Moses heard and wrote down the Almighty's words in Torah (Deut.31, 9 to 12). The Creator's spoken thoughts stored in Moses' Torah writings have authenticity only in their original Semitic context: that of the *ancient* language and Torah customs of its witnesses: Yeshua, a few gentiles and the Jewish people of the nation of Israel.

The circumstances of Torah's history and its Hebrew witnesses are also surviving signs of the Almighty's personal presence here on earth long ago. The trail to the Creator leads to the One Living God of certain ancient Semitic speaking peoples dwelling in the Middle East. These tribes of Semitic people have written documents tracing their descent from Adam down through Noah and his son Shem (a root of the word Semite) to Abram of Ur of the Chaldees, born 2166 B.C.E. (before

---

[4] *World Christian Encyclopedia. "Recently", as in the last twenty years as opposed to a time frame of 4,000 years of written history.*

the common era). From Abraham to Isaac to Jacob (a person renamed Israel by the Almighty) their descendants exist today as the nation of Israel. It is the nation of Israel alone who can trace their lineage to a time earlier than Noah back to the first descendants of Adam. No other present day nation or culture has a surviving detailed written family tree going back this far into prehistory. The writings of some nations have survived, but the peoples did not. Aboriginal peoples endure throughout the world today, but with large blanks in the details of their individual lineage. This extraordinary enduring of the descendants of Israel and their historical record beg us to examine the validity of their very old written claim that their One Living God watches over them. Their paleo writings contain the history of the Sayings of their One Living God which in the southern levant are dated from the middle bronze age forward into the iron age over a time period of a thousand years. Israel's pictographic writings disclose impressive details of the histories of their ancient tribes. They reveal the Almighty's ageless thinking as Torah documents His earliest Words first to their ancient ancestors (such as Noah and Abraham); Then to the genetic descendants of one man, Israel and to Moses both at Mount Horeb (Sinai) and over the ensuing forty years as the nation of Israel followed the Almighty's cloud wherever it led throughout desert lands. The chapters in this book were added over time as it dawned on me that these paleo writings are the only biblical sources we have which have not changed the Words in God's Speeches. On the basis of these circumstances and their Hebrew witnesses, the Semitic scripted Torah is the most compelling evidence of their One Living God. This is a book about Torah and Yehovah's Ways revealed, not about Judaism.

Hebrews for thousands of years have followed ingenious detailed rules to meticulously reproduce each and every symbol of Torah Scriptures in replacing old disintegrating copies of Torah. In modern society these days we are far too involved in a trendy pop culture of individual expression to pay any attention at all to Torah or to God's speeches to Israel. If it is thirty five hundred years old, it has to be hopelessly out of date, right? And so it is not accepted. It is cast aside, overlooked and even denigrated. But, **Torah is God's I.D. hidden in plain view.** The ancient Hebrews highly valued the origins or the beginning details of a person's life. They contain clues to the meaning or purpose of that person's life. The names of Hebrew individuals reflect these details of these origins. Yehovah is socially assumed. It should surprise no one when we find their Scriptures' very first words about God read, " *In the beginnings, Yehovah created...*" In the West, the beginnings of one's life are routinely neglected as a predictor suggesting one's life directions. Yehovah is not assumed as an active factor. A person's name is rarely chosen at birth on the basis of concurrent family events that foretell a person's future character. Few, very few even think in those terms. The nation of Israel centers its life on Yehovah.

Innovative interpretations of Scripture provided by foreigners routinely lead one in directions that repudiate fundamental thoughts of God, such as Do Not Change My Words and the pivotal Genesis 12, 3. If you are a gentile reader, you will find facts and conclusions throughout the book which differ from your view of Scriptures. This only means gentiles do not have a Semitic view of Semitic phenomena: the same view God chose in order to create Torah. It means gentiles do not know Torah. The end result of subjecting Torah to translation by foreign attitudes is the multitude of religious movements whose teachings have new, different meanings applied to the Words of Yehovah. This is how we find ourselves in the incubus of a nightmare we are experiencing today: 10,000 world wide religions and the 34,800+ denominations of Christianity,[5] each from one Torah.

God pointed out that to attempt to relate to Him on any basis other than the instructions in Torah is an abomination to Him.[6] In this book the phrase *relating to Him on any other basis* is the operational definition of RELIGION. **If it is not from Torah, it came from the mind of a human being**. God's own word abomination suggests that He "hates" or turns his Face away from human beings who changed His words and therefore the meaning of His teachings. There are other factors, but on its face, this explains the title of this book. This working definition of religion undoubtedly brings many questions to your mind, however I cannot tell you everything at once. Depending upon the extent to which you have practiced a religion, you will have certain misconceptions to replace. More practice equals more misconceptions.

Regarding commentary on the bible, how does one determine whose interpretation is "correct"? This is THE issue for ignorant foreigners like us. We don't know the language, the culture or the history. Here's what is happening: if an interpretation relies on a change in any way to the earliest Scriptures, that interpretation will fail to continue to explain later scriptures without also changing them. For its own survival it must change. And we do find that religion frequently solves this challenge by making use of abstractions, spiritualization and anachronisms (placing causal events earlier in a time in which they could not have existed). According to the Hebrew perspective adopted here, themes of the Almighty are His same Ways in Torah and in NT [7], from Genesis to Revelation. Differences in application may exist, but the reflected Ways of Yehovah remain from beginning to fulfillment. To survive, religions have created changes to God's earlier Torah in

---

[5] *World Christian Encyclopedia.*
[6] *Deuteronomy 18,9 Abomination= disgusting, foul, rotten experience?*
[7] *The terms Old v. New Testament reflect the way religion blindly replaces **Old** Writings with **New**. This is linguistic and functional Anti Semitism. Hebrew prose replaced in content and meaning with foreign sourced prose. Hence NT.*

order to later create *their* outcome: routinely, Hebrews are replaced by a given religion's people who then become God's people. Thus NT, ironically, could also signify "New Torah". Genesis 12, 3 prohibits antiSemitism, with teeth.

All of us judge unfamiliar information using our own personal criteria. We achieve these criteria as a result of our rational thought modified by relatively enduring tendencies developing in our minds as a result of personal experiences in our native culture: habits. Taken together your habits result in your view of the world. If you live in the western world you develop western habits, a western world view with its mindsets of interpretations and cultural values. The Hebrews developed their habits, mindsets and values based upon their ancient Semitic Torah Scriptures and their familial memories of Yehovah living among them in the land of Canaan. Yes, modern Hebrews have familial memories of the physical Presence of YHWH among their ancestors. It comes from a curious Torah inspired habit of teaching their children to periodically relive their ancestor s' personal experiences of God. This is how a Hebrew family functions during each of Yehovah's Holy Days or Feasts. It is God's plan to create in them authentic habits of understanding Him. These habits, the original stories of Torah and their ancestors' experiences are what they pass down through their generations and collectively constitute the modern Hebrews' perspective. For this reason, if we are searching for an authentic explanation of some ancient artifact found in the Holy Land we should search among the explanations offered by Hebrews who are experts in that field. Similarly, the authenticity of Hebrew commentary trumps the alternative ideas of foreigner's biblical commentary. In addition, Yehovah promised in Gen 12, 3 that anyone who injures or offends His chosen descendants of Abram through his descendant Israel or by implication His Torah, even His Holy Days, is subject to trouble, as in cursed by Yehovah. This book totally utilized Hebraic perspectives from Hebrew experts. Discussions of Judaism cannot be avoided. But tenets of Judaism were avoided, because the standard is Moses' written Torah.

Consider all of this and do not be lulled into arguments denigrating Y'israel. The only context of Torah for us foreigners is in the form of the experience and resulting knowledge and understanding of Yehovah and His Words possessed by the modern descendants of Israel. So, if one is paying attention Hebraically to Torah, then certain Scriptures stand out in particular as revealing the Almighty's thoughts about how human beings should relate to Him:

[I am going to bring disaster upon this people. It is the consequence of their own failure to pay attention to my words. And as for My Torah, they

ignore it].[8]

So there it is for all time! How Yehovah takes it when His Words are changed, ignored or rejected. So, do you personally ignore Torah, passover, and the six feasts of Yehovah? Aside from sharing Yehovah's expressed plans with you, there is no intention of proselytizing you with any religious agenda. Nor does this book intend to judge anyone for some presumed violation of Torah. I am not a rabbi. God has His own stated plan for making Himself completely known to everyone in the world, but men cannot wait for it so then religions have become mostly evangelical. My wish is that you will know His Ways and be able to say, "Hey, God didn't say that!", thus becoming immune to religious evangelism.

By extension the modern descendants or the "children of " Israel claim the blessings the Almighty gave to Abraham noted in Genesis 12, 3.

Now the Lord had said to Abram: "Get out of your country, from your kindred and from your fathers's house. (Go) **To a land that I will show you. I will make you a great nation; I will bless you and make your name great; And you shall be a blessing. I will bless those who bless you; And I will curse him who curses you; And in you all the families of the earth shall be blessed."**

It is not that Hebrews have claimed this blessing by their own opinion, but that the Almighty himself chose to extend His blessings for mankind through Abram's descendant the man Ya'akov (Jacob, Israel). The Hebrews have known this for 3500 years: one God, one people and one message. They have spent that time, among other pursuits, working out how an individual person should make each one of the Almighty's instructions a reality in the way they conduct their daily lives. This is the true meaning of **doctrine, it is personal conduct**. Differences among Hebrews interpreting Torah are to a very large degree related to the national loss of the Temple and Yehovah's Presence in it. Interpretations of Torah are the essence of life in Judaism. Studying Torah is the highest ideal a Hebrew man can achieve. After the destruction of the second Temple, the nation of Israel had no choice but to substitute study of Torah for the Temple worship practices. Torah and Temple are most sacred, but for the Hebrews only Torah presently remains a reality. To illustrate the weight of this point, an archaeological site some time ago unearthed a huge cast glass window with the exact dimensions needed to be installed in the Jerusalem Temple. It had been damaged during casting and so was never used for that purpose, being buried at the casting site. That site is now a highly sought burial site for those Hebrews able to afford it who wish their bones to be buried near anything related to Temple, even a broken man made object that was merely *intended* for use in the Temple. This is the **Hebraic Perspective** in action. Does any foreign religious

---

[8] Jeremiah 6,10b and 20.

group bury their loved ones there? We gentiles who wish to access the God of Israel have additional challenges. Not only is the Temple unavailable, Torah words are unfamiliar. While some highly motivated gentiles might eventually learn Hebrew and even ancient Hebrew, unless a Jewish perspective is personally embraced, the result of this effort will be more misguided changes to, and irrational theological explanations of Torah.

In Judaism the study of Torah occurs within the larger setting of all Hebraic scriptures notably the writings of the ancient rabbis such as the Mishnah published around the 3rd century B.C.E. It is full of interesting historical events. Some have said that twenty three hundred years of written Jewish interpretation and commentary are a change to Torah. That also may *appear* to be a religion as defined in this book. I am mostly ignorant of anything not written in English. I am not a rabbi. Who am I to make such accusations against Mishna or varieties of Judaism. Hebrew witnesses of Torah, even by a Karaite such as ancient Hebrew linguist Nehemia Gordon himself, often describe Scripture terms by including commentary identified as Rabbinic teachings. Who am I that I should decide which Hebrew commentary is or is not authentic witness of Torah? This paragraph again serves to delineate the boundary for this book which is only the written Torah of Moshe.

Few if any Christians have any idea how very little they follow Torah in comparison with Semitic peoples throughout the world who personally and intimately observe Torah, daily. On one side there is One God and one people living by Yehovah's One Torah. On the other, there are 34,800 named movements of Christianity with their own exclusive bibles, group names and customs. So religious reality today is the chaos of Multiples versus the order of One.

Sooner or later most people question if there is a Creator. Can that be demonstrated by a communication to us? While man made traditions in various Christian churches deflect their people from their own foundation of the Hebrew Scriptures, there is a route to the Almighty successfully taken by the ancient biblical figures Abraham, Noah and others long before Torah was written. These pathways were later elaborated in Torah. But, modern church founders erected false signposts directing the masses of faithful God seekers unwittingly away from the Almighty's holy path of Torah. It is necessary to highlight these false religious signposts throughout the book. It was not pleasing work. It was not meant to trash religion. When one deals with these false signposts individually and removes each from the equation, one achieves a baby step away from human religious plans and moves down the trail to Yehovah's Ways. This is the advantage of this book for the reader.

This book shines the light of day on religious teachings which dismiss Yehovah's Words, as we saw in the quote of Jeremiah 6, 10b and 20. *God Hates*

Religion does not vilify centuries of beautiful acts by beautiful people nor judge any religious individuals seeking God in good faith, rather it considers them to be its potential audience. In Numbers chapter 15 there are astonishing face to face discussions between Yehovah and Moses regarding the people's inability to follow Torah. Inability as opposed to Torah breaking actions that are defiant of Yehovah. Yehovah provided mercy without changing Torah. True God seekers, though unwittingly following any pagan teaching points in good faith that it they are pleasing the Almighty can know that Yehovah has in the past provided mercy for those trapped by life.

I am not fluent in Hebrew. For the purposes of this book, I do not have to be. You have here the authentic knowledge of Hebrew expert sources. Obviously, any reader is free to develop criteria and search out your own interpretations and sources as you wish. Be my guest. Maybe you will provide better questions and answers than you are reading here. At any rate as the first few books piled up, we wearied of wading through what other people had to say about God and desired to read the Scriptures in English but true to the original Semitic meanings. We found David H. Stern's **Complete Jewish Bible**. This bible was the first sign in English on the Hebraic path to the Almighty. However, its Christian NT does not have a Semitic roots translation. Its Introduction is especially helpful. The Jewish Publications Society offers *The Tanakh Holy Scriptures* and their ☞ **Jewish Study Bible** ☜ which is the Tanakh plus a side by side explanation of its significance by Hebrew experts. It is not a word for word English translation, it is the negotiated product of a group of very knowledgeable Hebrews. It is desirable because it provides us with a very rich Hebrew based commentary on Torah, in English. For some time now, it has been my bible. The **Jewish Study Bible** also provide us with some idea of the amazing breadth of the Jewish context of the bible, missing from western bibles. All other Jewish writings, such as the Christian NT are legitimately labeled post biblical scriptures meaning they are additions, written after Tanakh. For a Hebrew the bible is the Tanakh or Torah in the large sense. The Tanakh was Jesus' bible. Shouldn't it be yours? The NT, as taught by Christianity is not only a huge change to Tanakh, it is utilized to dismiss Torah. While both the written words of Jesus and implications of the Israelite perspective have led us to concur with this post biblical label for the NT, ALL these writings are the Hebrew's national heritage literature, their history.

We did not find a high fidelity translation of the NT, nor unquestioned Semitic NT manuscripts with the exceptions of Matthew and Hebrews. Nehemiah Gordon found an example of each in the ancient Hebrew!

Near the end of writing this book one more bible was reluctantly purchased. It was George Lamsa's **Holy Bible From the Ancient Eastern Text**. It has both the

Tanakh and the NT reproduced according to the same strict scribal sacred protocols as Torah. As a result all of its copies from various historical periods world wide agree with each other. An interesting feat and one that stands out as unique in the world wide history of NT translations. The fact is that the language spoken by the people featured in the NT was Aramaic. George Lamsa's NT is a translation into English directly from the Aramaic and by Lamsa himself who was a native speaker of Aramaic. His English phraseology however was from early 1930s Christianity. Lamsa was a Christian. For almost two thousand years men have incorrectly pled that these NT writings were **originally** written down in Greek. Hence seminaries have taught budding clergy the Greek language for as long as there have been seminaries. It seems that the Aramaic language may be another small quiet fact historically overlooked by most everyone. With all this talk about bibles, you should not lose sight of the fact that this book does not have a goal of converting anyone to a religion. Rather it seeks to demonstrate how everyone should be immune to religious proselytizing.

There were many challenges in collecting information relevant to the theme of this book. A half dozen English language bibles emerged from three of the broad religious classifications descended from the God of the Semites Abraham, Isaac and Israel: namely Judaism, Christianity and the Messianics whose writings *currently* derive mostly from Christianity. However, Messiah is inherently and originally Semitic. Many if not all Hebrews frame their future in Messiah.

The bibles and commentary books cited in this book were the best Semitic sourced ancient Scriptures in English available in my research timeline for someone seeking the bible's Hebrew roots. In addition there are many quotes from traditional English Christian bibles in this book, some of which you will find illustrate believers following a tradition which is obviously false even when stated in their own Greek sourced Latinized English bible! Since English bibles are generally written from a particular religious tradition, each also has its own take on what constitutes the Semitic perspective. Some completely discount it. If we define a tradition as a pattern of action based upon a group ethic or value system which is inherited by default and originates from an earlier or higher source, then in this book traditional Christian values are presented as the default inheritance of native English, for which Moses' written Torah is the earlier and higher source.

If you want pure Torah in English, get one like that provided by The Jewish Publication Society. All of the English NT versions examined are nonSemitic and they substitute inaccurate, misleading English terms that systematically misrepresent the underlying Semitic words, many of them connected to Torah. The first clue about this came from Nehemiah Gordon's truly excellent book **The Hebrew Yeshua vs. The Greek Jesus**. Here you will find displayed a number of inaccurate Torah terms in the English including instances of missing words and context violations, some of which affect how Yeshua is characterized. So, *your* trail also leads to Nehemiah Gordon's book. Sadly the Lamsa bible's translation does not escape these linguistic dilemmas in spite of its Aramaic origin. It's choice of English words came from the Christian jargon of the 1930s. This revives a characteristic method of false biblical justification of the Christian faith, to wit anachronisms, placing some event or causal explanation earlier in a time in which it could not have existed. For example, if you say the word bible while speaking of Jesus' time, it is not the NT. The only bible you can be referencing is the Tanakh. It was the bible of Jesus. The NT had yet to be written. Many Christian speak anachronistically as though Jesus was aware of the NT writings. He was not. They did not exist during his lifetime.

In this book at times a Hebraic perspective of Torah Words is offered as paraphrase enclosed by brackets [ ]. I almost hate doing this, but it is for demonstration purposes only. This does not add words to Scripture but explains Semitic perspective. These bracketed offerings are not translations because both the texts used in the paraphrase are in English. A translation involves going from a foreign source language to a different target language. Brackets indicate the Hebrew perspective's significance of that word. Often the only word changed is that of the Name of the Almighty. We are trying to illustrate the original meaning of His Words. Again, I am not fluent in Semitic languages; For this book, I do not have to be. What guides any paraphrasing then is the enlightenment of the Hebrew perspective with its emphasis on fidelity to the Torah's plain words. Here's an example:

Most names for God are words that refer to some characteristic that He possesses. They are not what He calls Himself, which is a word that truly is His Name. The first individual to know the actual Name of the Almighty according to God's plain words is Moshe. Here is Exodus 6, 2 and 3 in the NKJV: **"And God spoke to Moses and said to him: 'I am the Lord, I appeared to Abraham, to Isaac, and to Jacob, as God Almighty, but by My name Lord I was not known to them.'"** Does any person seriously think that the Almighty really said to Moses "My Name is Lord?" Here is the paraphrased version that is true to its Hebraic roots: **[God spoke to Moshe and He said to him, I am Yehovah]** (realize that later, *after* this conversation took place, Moses wrote God's Name as yod, hei, vav, hei; 𐤉𐤄𐤅𐤄 Yehovah). **[I appeared to Avraham, to Yitz'chak and to Ya'akov as El Shaddai.**[9]

---

[9]*An old Canaanite name for their god. It took about 200 years for the Israelites to conquer Canaan and apparently God allowed this usage of His name for some time. Another Canaanite term Elyon referred to a local god.*

But by My Name Yehovah was I not known to them.[10]] Now doesn't that make the New King James Version sound ridiculous? In the actual conversation He did not say His Name is "Lord". He said it is *Yod Hei Vav Hei*, Yahweh or Yehovah. You may be thinking, "Okay, so now I know His Name, so what? I believe a person should be able to call God by whatever word they like." If that is your idea, you do realize we are talking about the Almighty King of the Universe, right? WAKE UP! You are saying something that grinds on the Almighty, why not stop misquoting Him? There is another reason to avoid this misquotation. In Psalm 91, the psalmist addresses his audience in the first person urging them to abide in their trust of YHWH so that no harm will befall them. The last three verses are spoken in a different voice as God's reply to the psalmist's words and the reply affirms His protection of the psalmist but for a reason, a reason not based upon trust. From Psalm 91, 14b we have God's final word: **"because he knows my name, I will protect him".**[11] Men blindly advocate faith, but this Psalm tells us that YHWH values and acts upon the specific knowledge of His Name.

In describing the Creator's Sayings in Torah, the point of reference of this book had to jump back and forth between three religious groups: Christian, Judaism and Messianic. Since a term or interpretation may be nonexistent in one group, a researcher has to find information from among others which do incorporate the phenomenon. Each of these three is convinced the others are incorrect in their understanding of scriptures and in their practices. The present Hebraic survey of Torah also reflects the author's personal longing to find the Almighty's thoughts accurately explained in English. We should not be bound by a religion to understand the words of Yehovah, as they all have their agendas. The Hebrew perspective of Yahweh's written Torah of Moshe is the only avenue presently available to English speaking gentiles for truly understanding YHWH's thinking. If you try to use the NT for that purpose you will be led astray. **You may feel that Torah set up the religion of Judaism, so that in fact Christianity is being judged by Judaism. No, the standard is not Judaism but Torah.** YHWH spoke Torah as His instructions detailing how Israel should occupy His land and how the nation of Israel should worship Him in that land. His Plan was for Israel to be His priests, witnessing His Name and unchanged Torah to foreigners throughout earth. Torah, the written form of Yehovah's speeches, is a creation of the mind of Yehovah and is quite beyond our definition of man made religions. So we, bound by religion are freed by Torah.

---

[10]*Exodus 6, 2 and 3. I checked the Modern Semitic text in the Hebrew English bible and found that it says YHWH or yod, hei, vav, hei. So for us living in these times, that is His acknowledged Name. It means "I am, I will be what I will be".*
[11]*In times of personal trouble, you can dial 911 as it were, by going to Psalm 91,1 and praying or meditating all 16 verses.*

Prologue

In the USA, the mighty Mississippi river begins as crystal clear spring waters flowing into Lake Itasca, Minnesota. The river and what happens to its water on its journey to the sea is an allegory for the effect of human religious traditions on the Creator's Torah. The Mississippi terminates twenty-three hundred miles downstream into the Gulf of Mexico near New Orleans, Louisiana, USA. At that point it is no longer pristine water, but very, muddy and contaminated. Drinking it directly would be the last thing on your mind. The source of the contamination is not at its beginnings, *there* the water is perfect. It picks up bits of foreign material throughout its long journey as it passes by human activities: every city, town, factory and farm. What began as healthful and refreshing spring water now carries accumulated debris discharged into it for human convenience. It has been changed into contaminated water by people along its banks who use the river for their own purposes. For best health, human beings as well as fish and aquatic mammals require pure water with nothing else added. Ironically, you can stand today at the ocean end of the Mississippi and realize that hidden there in the water you see is the exact same pure water flowing from its origin. Human activities have added to the pure water so that now it is unfit for human consumption.

Thirty five hundred years ago, the Almighty spoke the crystal clear Words of life by which He meant human beings to thrive. Now, all these centuries later these life giving Words have flowed down to us past hundreds of generations of human input which have added foreign ideas to the Words of His Torah. The original significance of His Words is now diluted with human religious plans. Humans have tweaked His Torah for their own purposes. The tweaks have altered the plans conveyed to us in God's Sayings. A myriad of religious activities over many generations mislead God seekers as to the true ancient Ways of Yehovah.

Chapter 1

God Gave Speeches to the Hebrews?

How do we know that the Almighty gave Torah in speeches to the Israelites? It could be that the Israelites made up Torah via their own culturally generated legends.

In the mid 1960s I took a physical science course at Westmont College in California. I can only recall one part of the course. In that part, Professor Emeritus Peter W. Stoner demonstrated the mathematical improbabilities of dozens of prophecies found in ancient writings of Middle Eastern Semites. For each prophesied event he demonstrated the computed probabilities of its fulfillment and each one emerged astronomically against it ever being fulfilled. The point of this teaching was that each prophesied event HAD subsequently come true years later in historical fact. In fact, the prophecies all came from the ancient Hebrew writings called Tanakh. Recalling them all these years later, the impact of the consummated prophecies of Tanakh still inspires me. To illustrate the level of improbability of each prophesied event, here is a test prophecy for you: what are the odds you could correctly predict the next twelve large, thriving cities in the USA to cease to exist in the near future? Gnarly, isn't it?

Since learning about those dozens of unlikely but fulfilled prophecies, a fret has run for many years in the back of my mind that God has orchestrated something BIG right in front of us, yet we are not dealing with it (Jeremiah 10b, 20 again). In more than a half century hearing sermons from various church pulpits, how often did I hear of these historically validated prophecies? NEVER! There is something important here that Christianity has traditionally dismissed. Sad to say, we humans have a tremendous capability for creatively modifying the facts and import of events in our own history.[12] In the case of validated Hebrew prophecies, that is not so. It would have been better to present you with the actual Physical Science class data. These data are presently not available to me. After 48 years, this is the only specific undergraduate college teaching I remember.

However I do recall Dr. J. Vernon McGee and the week he spoke at Westmont's Chapel. Attendance tripled, people hung from the chandeliers and on his every teaching point. Years later, during my corporate traveling years, his Through the Bible radio show was a true Godsend. Eventually I acquired the 5 volume hardbound book set of his radio teachings which provided for family bible studies during middle aged years. A frequent and knowledgeable visitor and fan of the land of Israel, he was fluent in Hebrew. Occasionally, Dr. McGee would launch a "tirade" against the Christian world for failing to respect Israel and the Hebrew roots of the faith. I came to believe he was frustrated at *almost* making a better connection himself. This observation stayed with me and undoubtedly provided a basis for my fascination with Israel and Torah.

So, there are these unique fulfilled prophecies. Our habits prevent us from recognizing what our eyes see and our ears hear. You may recall how it is when you have lost some item. Cannot find it. Then, like magic it appears in a place you have already searched. It is a perceptual anomaly; *Or,* we may ask the Almighty, " How did You do that?" The point is very often the answer to a mystery can be found later on to have been in one's face the entire time. There is plenty of written and archeological evidence left to us by the Almighty pointing to the unique nature of His intervention into human history. This evidence has a tangible, practical concreteness about itself. It can be easily understood within its Hebraic context as it speaks for itself, if one takes care not to explain it away, out of context.

The trail to the Almighty leads us to Torah. When old Hebrew prophecies become history, they validate the Almighty's authorship not only of the prophecies but also of all the writings (Tanakh) in which Hebraic prophecies are found. The earliest and most sacred part of the Tanakh Scriptures is the first five scrolls[13] known as *Torah*. The word Torah also is generically used by many to refer to *Tanakh*. Beginning around the first century of the common era (C.E.), the five scrolls began to be scribed together on one scroll. Torah contains God's timeless instructions to humanity. Yehovah's Torah covers worship practices, civil or government practices and personal behavior. Taken together, these fulfilled prophecies are heavy objective

---

[12]*Hegel's Paradox: Man learns from history that man learns nothing from history.*
[13] *A continuous roll of writing medium, not cut up into pages.*

evidence that the Hebrews did not just make up Torah from their own minds.

Many of us are unable to read any Semitic language and are unable to travel or live in the Holy Land, but wish to learn of the Living God of Israel without all the drama of religion. Not listed in the Bibliography are many other promising books which failed to facilitate this Semitic search for the Almighty's thinking. Their trails led nowhere, or in circles. Since quite a bit of the information that could shape our attitudes about God's message comes from various sources of antiquities, attention was paid to the nation of Israel's archaeological artifacts. When presented with differing explanations about artifacts whose authenticity is not questioned, one should choose an Israelite view of Israelite artifacts. From Simca Jocobovici's entertaining and thoroughly Hebraic television series, *The Naked Archaeologist*, I found that one's understanding of most biblical antiquities discovered in the Holy Land or any other middle eastern country is dependent upon one's knowledge of the Hebrew Scriptures. Similarly, a Scripture will take on new meaning when one realizes that a given Scriptures' contention is validated by the artifact at hand. If we do not care about Scriptures, then the meaning of some important artifacts will be lost on us. Nowhere is that more true than in the case of ancient cave writings found in Egypt showing lines of paleo Hebrew letters, which we are alerted to in Simca's work. This is Hebrew paleo graffiti found at an indentured worksite in a remote cave in Egypt. Some four hundred years before written Torah, a Canaanite worker pleaded with EL, ⌐ in the ancient paleo Hebrew character, to not forget him. This fascinating finding, proto Sinaitic writing, demonstrates the Hebrews could write their own language prior to the giving of Torah at Mt. Sinai. You can read the article for yourself in the Journal **Biblical Archaeology Review**, March/April 2010, Vol. 36 No 2. entitled **"How the Alphabet was born from Egyptian Hieroglyphs"** by Professor Orly Goldwasser. It is available at www.biblicalarchaeology.org. Throughout Torah the Almighty restates the fact that the Canaanite god known as EL refers to Himself at a time before His Name was known to mankind. ⌐ thus refers to the One and Only Yehovah.

Chapter 2

The Hebrews Still Face Us

Two factors validate the need to search for an accurate aboriginal knowledge of the Almighty's Torah. The first is the nagging problem, described in Chapter 1, of explaining how all those ancient Hebrew prophecies came true so many years after their predictions were written down. The second is dealing with the continued existence of the Israelite people on earth and in the same highly contested lands they claim as ancestral. All the other ancient "ites" in those Middle East lands are extinct. Thus there are no other living peoples who can legitimately claim ancestral links to the land of Israel which predate the modern nation of Israel. Even the mighty Egyptians are totally extinct, including their language and their alphabet. Modern day peoples of Egypt are immigrants who came from other Middle Eastern lands and are settlers who merely filled in the rich lands vacated by the extinct ancient Egyptians. In ancient times Egypt and the other now extinct mideastern cultures were all far larger and more powerful than Israel. Yet Israel endures: a consequence promised by Yehovah in Gen, 12, 3, *et.al.*

Together these two facts put us on notice that we must take most seriously the Israelite ancestral claim to have personally heard the voice of the Almighty and received His blessing. The present day direct lineal descendants of these ancient Israelites are the modern eyewitnesses to the world's greatest historical event, which is the Presence of the Almighty *dwelling* among them here on earth. The modern eyewitness claim is not merely my opinion, nor the opinion of Jewish people, rather it is demonstrated throughout Scriptures to be the design of the Almighty. The basis of this claim is established not only by their continued presence in the land of Israel, but also by their Torah observance of reliving Yehovah's presence as a method of child rearing. This child rearing practice endows each succeeding generation with their common ancestral knowledge of Yehovah. While many western foreigners utilize churches for aspects of the task of "godly" child rearing, Torah delegates this responsibility to the family. In the place of learning of Yehovah's interaction with one's ancestors from one's mother and father via historical recitations of the history of each of Yehovah's Feasts and holy days, children in western religions impersonally learn a theologically enhanced foreigners' story from pastors and other church leaders. The point is that Hebraic ancestral reliving of the Presence and Sayings of the Almighty here on earth has been largely dismissed by the world's religions who dismiss history and lead their followers to *spiritual* training. However Yehovah highly values individuals who live by family honor, the 5th commandment is the only one with a promised reward. See also chapter 10, Salvation, #3. Meanwhile, nations come and go, but only Y'israel endures. We could conclude that for Yehovah, there is no other point at issue: Y'israel endures. That is why they matter. Consider human ideas of spirituality taught to children by western gentile Christian church leaders. Since western Christian leaders have no documented history of the Almighty physically dwelling among them in the New World, they default into reenactment of holy land events including as *poseurs* or actors posing as Yehovah's appointed priests. As time passes individuals who are in self appointed roles as actors create their own new realities which *they* label as holy. They would do anything except carry or even touch the ark of the covenant. And that is their situation. The ark WAS holy, having in it the Presence of Yehovah. Instant death to anyone who touched it except for Yehovah's genetically appointed cohenim or priests, people nowadays surnamed Cohen. If you have a prop of the ark, then obviously anyone can touch it. Take the church's *reenactment* of the communion supper. It is a dismissive alternative for observing any feast of Yehovah. The phrase "as oft as you do this" in the NT's Last Supper account refers to the six Torah Feasts; These six Feasts are observed by virtually no Christian church.

    The bedrock of Yehovah's Words and His Name is literally in Israel, not America. Throughout history and in many lands, the teachings of the Christian church have continuously changed. By definition, bedrock does not change. It is the secure foundation. That statement seems obvious, however religions routinely fool their people by making small changes over time. Only Israel has the secure foundation of YHWH's Presence among them dwelling on land He claimed for Himself. We want to believe in the Christian stories of Christ because it all seems so worthwhile. But the ideas of churches are in a 2,000 year old state of flux. We are all gullible. These bedrock Christian principles are *at best* ghosts of Torah. As will be abundantly described throughout this book, the only bedrock is the Almighty's Torah. The teachings of the western gentile Christian church are abstractions which do not exist in the plain written Words of the Holy One of Israel. The pure water, is to be found at the beginning of the river in the form of YHWH's written Torah of Moshe. Sadly religions continue to cause their followers to look for the answers at the wrong end of the river. It will not always be so, you could change now.

Ironically Torah is the Scriptures that even Christianity itself acknowledges to be their foundation. What has gone wrong? Almost all Christians have always been taught by their church that their NT scriptures were written in Greek.[14] But, all the writings in the Christian church's bible, both NT and Torah were originally spoken and then later written down in Hebrew and Aramaic. Both languages use the same symbolic aleph beit. Greek translations of the NT are foreign changes introduced for the convenience of religion builder's goals. Starting with the Greek Septuagint translation of Torah in 275 B.C.E., foreign language translations of Torah have been utilized by Hebrews throughout the ages with the historical Hebrew Torah text presented alongside on each page! But, two centuries later, NT translations into Greek began *replacing* the original Aramaic writings but did not present them alongside the new Greek translation. This is suspicious considering the original ancient Hebrew Matthew safely stored in Israel and casts doubt upon the fidelity of Greek translations. So here is the situation. This is where the bear sleeps:

The English NT's overall theme of faith suddenly appears with the Greek translations of the four Gospel books. However the theme of Torah observance pervades Jesus' teachings throughout the ancient Hebrew Matthew. Living by faith was added by Greek translation skewing attention away from Jesus' missing theme of living by Torah. Jesus was a Hebrew not a Greek.

Greek myths also influenced choices of words for biblical translations. One appears much later into the 1600s C.E. King James English. In Genesis 6, 4, the story of mankind's early life on earth has embedded in it this nugget in English: *"There were giants on the earth in those days, and also afterward, when the sons of God came in to the daughters of men and they bore children to them...."* The actual Hebrew word is not giants but *nephilim*. According to Professor Gerald Schroeder, The Hebrew University, the word Nephilim means fallen ones in the sense of being lower or subhuman. How did this incorrect English word giant find its way into translations of Torah? The Greeks had an elaborate system of mythological characters. One was the myth of Titans. Their own myths about a giant race of titans influenced their translation of the word *nephilim*. By the 1600s when the *Latinized* Greek Torah Septuagint was being translated into the King James English version, the word *nephilim* had been completely replaced by the substitute word giant, finally validating Greek mythology regarding Titans. Your Christian bible then has bogus Greek mythology in it. The biblical term *nephilim* is factually affirmed by the fact

---

[14] *If the NT' was originally written in Greek, why do Hebrew puns, plays on sounds of Hebrew words appear in "original" Greek? They are translations.*

that human DNA, that is of *homo sapiens*, has up to 5% Neanderthal DNA (*nephilim*) depending upon racial ancestry. See *Nephilim*, Ch 10. The point is that our English NT translations are inaccurate.

A Hebraic Perspective: the Power of Yehovah's Words

Throughout the ages millions of people have taken comfort in the beautiful words of the twenty third psalm. It's allegorical meaning is relatively easy for even an English speaking city dweller to understand since most people should be able relate to the idea that a shepherd works hard to create a good life for his flock of sheep. Less well understood is the very first Psalm. The theme of Psalm 1 describes the consequences of accepting or rejecting Torah. Psalm 1 says in the New King James version:

"Blessed is the man who walks not in the counsel of the ungodly, nor stands in the path of sinners, nor sits in the seat of the scornful. But his delight is in the law of the Lord and in His law he meditates day and night. And he shall be like a tree planted by the rivers of water that brings forth its fruit in its season, whose leaf also shall not wither. And whatsoever he does shall prosper. The ungodly are not so but are like the chaff which the wind drives away. Therefore the ungodly shall not stand in the judgement, nor sinners in the congregation of the righteous. For the Lord knows the way of the righteous, but the way of the ungodly shall perish."

Notice that Torah is not even mentioned! After you have read this book and learned an appreciation for the Hebrew perspective of the Almighty's Words, the following wording describes how you might understand the thinking in Psalm 1 using English thoughts.[15] You will find that Psalm 1 is truly how a person was meant to live life upon this earth. Everyone should know that Torah is Yehovah's plan for a beautiful life on earth; It is the freedom solution to human life on earth; And it was intended to be conveyed to all mankind via Israel. Here is the Torah observant lifestyle described with Hebraic perspective:

[A happy life is experienced by anyone who avoids advice from those oblivious to Torah and by anyone who avoids conducting their life swayed by the thinking of man made traditions. Rather their joy of life is Yehovah's Torah. This truly fulfilled person centers his life on Yehovah's Torah and Torah occupies his mind day and night. Because of this practice he possesses deep roots intertwined with thoughts from the Almighty and this benefits him throughout his life. His character increases rather than diminishes and his activities bring him good not harm. On the opposite side are those who have rejected the Almighty's Words and so are doomed to be victimized by the chaos in their lives. Because of this choice, Torah deficient people will not prevail in the coming great day of judgement nor will

---

[15]*My paraphrase: rephrasing is not a translation. Both source and target texts are English; Words are chosen for perspective and I use "fatter" words.*

followers of man made religions be admitted to the gathering of those made righteous by their love of Torah. For Yehovah communes with those who observe His Words, but those who have dismissed His Words will have nothing.]

With this example of Yehovah's Psalm 1 thinking in mind, how then is a person to live life in harmony with God? If you are looking for what personal practices God requires of you, it is available in His words courtesy of Rabbi Mordecai Alfandari. Titled ***The Way of YHWH***, it lists nineteen groups of Torah instructions that apply to everyone. It can be found in the "Light of Israel" section at the World Karaite website at www.KaraiteKorner.org. Oddly, the website's copy is provided in old King James English. When you have read these scriptures enough you will begin to have in your mind the Almighty's original intentions for the nation of Israel. Then you, like me, can declare war on religion (no violence suggested, only intellectual war). **Problem**: Torah instructions apply to the descendants of the man Israel, the children or nation of Israel. What about the rest of us gentiles?

We gentiles may claim we foreigners are sojourners[16] with Israel and desire to follow the true path of Torah leading to the knowledge and worship of their God. This is Yehovah's mechanism to follow (become known by) Yehovah. Being personally unknown by Yehovah is troubling. The beginnings of this stranger sojourner route to God are found in Abraham's experience finding Yehovah while traveling through distant lands where he identified himself as both a stranger and a sojourner. And, Abraham, the Babylonian city dweller (Ur of the Chaldees) was a polytheist prior to encountering Adonai. Poetic beauty, no? He did not always know that Yehovah is the single individual Creator! He was a wanderer and a stranger in foreign lands. Sojourners are identified in Torah as foreigners who resided and identified with the nation of Israel and who chose to leave Egypt, travel with Israel and observe Torah requirements: notably the keeping (eating) of the Passover Feast. Now that the ten northern tribes (House of Israel) are spread out all over the world, it is not crystal clear if to qualify as a sojourner WE would have to move to the land of Israel. Detailed information is found at www.KaraiteKorner.org newsletter # 508 from Nehemiah Gordon. There is Scriptural basis for the gentile hope that personally identifying with Israel by observing Torah are sufficient to identify a gentile as a sojourner, thus <u>individually known by Yehovah</u>. Isaiah 56 says in Yehovah's Name:

[The son of the stranger who follows Yehovah should not say that I Yehovah have separated him from My people. And for the son of strangers who follow Me and love My Name, to be My servants and who keep from profaning My Sabbath and hold to My covenant, I will bring them to My holy mountain and I will give them joy in My house of prayer. Their offerings and their

---

[16]*Numbers 9, 10-14: sojourners and Passover; Numbers 15, 13-16: sojourner offerings. This is Yahweh's path for gentiles to follow His Ways.*

sacrifices shall be accepted on My altar. For My house shall be called the house of prayer for all nations.]

Churches love to quote only that last sentence while totally ignoring all the wonderful promises of blessings to gentiles who live as described here. We see that these blessings are also promised to the *descendants* of Yehovah's gentile sojourners, who continue their ancestor's sojourner ways. Our salvation, being known by Yehovah is justified by Isaiah 56, let us live by Torah, the ancient pathway to God.

More action for gentiles is found in Deuteronomy 27, 19 which says there is a curse on anyone who violates the rights of strangers, orphans and widows. Sojourners begin as strangers to Israel. In Deuteronomy 32, 43:

"Rejoice, O Gentiles with His people; For He will avenge the blood of His servants, And render vengeance to His adversaries; He will provide atonement for His land and His people."

On this subject (sojourners) and many other issues we gentiles all have need of someone to teach us Torah. Looking for someone to fulfill that function, one branch of Judaism, certain Karaites, are found to not appear to be involved in excess financial benefit, do not proselytize, and accept as holy only to the written Torah of Moshe. Indeed they have provided modern humanity with the present day pristine copies of Torah. Karaite and ancient Semitic linguist Nehemiah Gordon has been making his impressive skills, experience and knowledge of paleo Torah writings freely available to English speaking gentile audiences. Nehemiah Gordon's book **The Hebrew Yeshua vs. the Greek Jesus** is what you should read after you finish this book. Incredibly, his speaking activities have accrued negative feedback from both Judaism and Christianity. Scholars proposing solutions which transcend both sides of a social issue are often demonized by those whose agenda is at risk.[17]

The Tanakh Scriptures throughout promote a return to ancient ways (Jeremiah 6,16). Even modern Christian believers tend to describe their modern beliefs in the same terms used by the ancients even though the two sets of beliefs are highly incompatible. A case in point is the church's habit of referring to all believers from the present time back through to the first century believers as *Judeo Christians*. It also refers to its own teachings as Judeo Christian. This term is casually used as if it is 1,000 % true, however it could not be less descriptive of the true circumstances. There is nothing Judeo about current Christian beliefs. Everything Judaic has been systematically removed from Christian bibles and church teachings. All the first century followers of Jesus from the first fishermen chosen were thrilled to follow Rabbi Yeshua's ways which were to live solely by the provisions of the written

---

[17]*Benford's Law applies to the demonizers: Passion in any argument is inversely proportional to the level of substantive information offered.*

Torah of Moshe. These *talmidim* (students) were overjoyed to find relief from the heavy burden of ancient rabbinic Judaism and to find freedom in Yeshua's teaching of the Torah observant lifestyle. They loved incorporating the heart of Judaism (the Torah) into their daily lives. Yeshua and his followers kept the Sabbath on the seventh day of the week (a day later changed by a new tradition to the first day of the week, called Sun day in honor of Constantine's sun god *Sol Invictus Mithra*). Yeshua and his talmidim wore tzit tzit or white fringes on their garments with one blue thread. They obeyed worship instructions for the six feasts of Adonai and all Torah described holy days. And they specifically avoided gentiles completely including gentile languages. Their daily prayer life included the *Sh'ma* three times a day (affirming that Yehovah is one God alone). They were obedient only to Torah. All of these practices are what modern Torah observant Hebrews world wide practice daily. These Torah practices were also those of Yeshua, who may have been the first Karaite.[18] His surviving first generation followers, here referred to as *Yeshuaites*, continued his Torah practices after his passing. The Yeshuaites were the Jerusalem apostles whom the NT identifies as those receiving the Holy Spirit. They obeyed Torah. Any modern Christian can replicate Yeshua's Torah observant lifestyle.

After Yeshua left this earth, his followers continued his teachings of Judaic Torah practices led by James, Yeshua's brother, as well as Peter. James' *Yeshuaite* operation was headquartered in Jerusalem. It was in the same building which housed the upper room where the "last supper" was held. The apostles gathered there after Yeshua's crucifiction. It was THE upper room famously identified in Acts as the place receiving the Ruach Ha Kodesh (Holy Spirit). The Jerusalem based Yeshuaite movement came to an end by the year 70 of the common era (CE) when Roman soldiers totally destroyed Jerusalem and scattered its inhabitants. If you read the first five books of your Christian NT, these Judaic foundations of the history of Yeshua and his followers are strangely missing from the accounts. How can you reconcile the facts that Yeshuaite Torah observant practices **were sufficient to result in the receiving of the Ruach Ha Kodesh (Holy Spirit), but not sufficient for inclusion in the NT?** More details near the end of the book. For now our concern should be that since Jesus taught Torah, our hunt for the content of the real messages from God must lead us back to times before Yeshua.

The meaning of each written character symbol in the Hebrew language reflects a national psyche which compounds the Israelites' physical life in the created world with the overpowering reality of their firsthand experience of the Almighty's Presence among them 3500 years ago. It's in every letter of their language. You and

---

[18] *Observation by N. Gordon, The Hebrew Yeshua Versus the Greek Jesus.*

I have not had this firsthand experience in our ancestral heritage. We have not experienced God that way. That is not the fault of God, it is the plan of God. Also, these two Semitic languages, while inherently simple and elegantly concise, are richer than English. The goal for this book is to be a blessing to all readers directly from the Almighty's Semitic rooted words of Torah. Consider the experience of standing at an opened window when a sudden burst of cool, fresh air comes in so that you take a step back, throw up your hands and inhale deeply. This represents the Semitic experience of God. It is described in one paleo Semitic letter which is hei: ⚹. Is there a single letter in Greek or English which has this kind of descriptive power? The common alphabet (*aleph beit*) of these two Semitic languages is uniquely designed to truly bring the experience of God into our minds. I recall being taught in church that the Greek language is the one language uniquely configured to describe the spiritual things of God. Years later, I found that to be wrong: Greek has historically been the international language of philosophy and commerce. Greek was developed by humans to facilitate success with business activities, and to create realities out of abstract conceptual constructs which (*constructs*) do not exist in the physical. But the Hebrew language depends upon concrete objects and down to earth relationships to demonstrate the Ways of God which require action, not thinking. To experience Yehovah requires action. For example the letter hei: be at the window, and experience Yehovah by performing the ⚹ maneuver.

The Hebrew perspective is the obscure gem that is overlooked by all other nations and religions which have attempted in vain to adapt the Israelite experience with the Almighty to their own culture. The Hebrew's stories are relatively pointless without the Israelite perspective and therefore available for reinterpretation by foreigners. Yehovah's Words are explained in Semitic terms. The terms contain intrinsic reflections of the symbolic power of Hebrew and Aramaic. Religions change Yehovah's terms, gutting their power in order to substitute **their** people for the Jews as God's beneficiaries. This exact substitution has occurred repeatedly throughout history in many nations.

Context [19] is everything. To translate without becoming a liar, one should take the optional meanings, puns and all other literary embellishments of Torah's words intact to the new targeted language (English). Creating foreign language "equivalent" terms as substitutes not only clouds understanding it creates conditions ripe for the development of divergent human traditions. It changes Torah. It contradicts the Almighty's choice of terms in conveying His thinking to us.

---

[19]*Literally, " with the writing"*

Chapter 3
The Pagan Roots
of Christianity

This chapter provides details of some of the historical developments that religions borrowed to construct religious customs and traditions which herd people away from the Torah of Yehovah.

The following historical facts and myths reveal how three peoples separated by hundreds, even thousand of years have used the same pagan artifacts for different purposes in three different religions. The objects therefore cannot reasonably be regarded as given to us as "holy" by Yehovah. The following descriptions include both historical fact and historical mythology. This is a very short review as there are VOLUMES written about these subjects. This section describes the pagan roots of the gentile Christian religion.

Jupiter. In 255 B.C.E. a Syrian Greek general named Antioches Epipheny occupied Jerusalem. On the Temple Mount he set up a brass statue of the Greek god Jupiter. He declared Jupiter to be God. On that day, the winter solstice, December 25th, the general threw a birthday party for Jupiter and roasted a pig on the sacrificial altar on the Temple Mount. Prompted by this defilement of Yehovah's holy altar, the sons of Maccabees, who were in fact Israelite priests, made war on the general and three years later somehow prevailed against the heavy opposition of the general's army. The sons of Maccabees set up a new altar which was consecrated over an eight day period. This became the Jewish religious holiday known as Hanukkah (remembering the dedication of a new altar). All of this happened in the short period of time between the end of the writing of the Tanakh and the beginning events of the NT. Remember the brass statue.

Constantine. Outside St. Peter's Cathedral in Rome there is a statue of the Roman emperor Constantine seated on a war horse. Just before the battle of Milvian Bridge on October 28th, 312 C. E., Constantine knelt at sunrise just prior to his battle with the opposing Roman emperor Maxentius. Facing the sunrise on his knees, Constantine prayed to the Roman sun god Mithra. He was in imminent danger of losing his part of the Roman empire. As the sun rose, Constantine reported seeing a sign in the configuration of a cross as he squinted against the rising sunshine. He reported hearing a voice which said, "*In this sign conquer.*" He instantly realized the solution to his predicament and gave the order for his troops to swab a white cross on each shield. So equipped, his army was victorious and Maxentius drowned in the Tiber river near the entrance to Rome. Constantine proceeded to consolidate his newly expanded empire by incorporating all religions in his new lands under a new empire wide government religion called Christianity. This decree happened overnight and without a single personal religious conversion. Prior to all this, history tells us that Constantine dearly loved his mother who herself routinely worshiped with other believers as a Christian. She practiced Christianity during a time when it was a capital crime in Constantine's empire. All evidence shows that Constantine remained a worshiper of the Roman sun god *Sol Invictus Mithra* for his entire life. In Constantine's mind Christianity was a tool for preserving his empire *and* he loved his mother. He implemented his new empire consolidation tool by declaring that anyone who keeps the Jewish Sabbath would be killed. (Note that in Torah Yehovah calls it My Sabbath). No Feasts of the Jews (Torah calls them Yehovah's Feasts) were allowed to be practiced. If there were any Torah observant Yeshuaites left after Shaul took control of their Jerusalem based operation three hundred years earlier, this certainly finished them. In the place of Sabbaths and Feasts, Constantine approved pagan feasts, holidays and holy days. These pagan days were given new Christian names. For example in the place of the pagan observance of a day for the goddess Ishtar, the day became Easter. Aspects of Ishtar worship were merged with Christian memorial worship patterns. The birthday of Tammuz, who was the Mithra christ, was moved to Christmas day. All religious activities in the conquered lands were consolidated under "Christianity". Constantine executed anyone found to be keeping Jewish Sabbaths or Jewish holy days. In fact he got rid of everything Jewish: not only the Torah's holy days but also replaced the Jewish Messiah with the christ called Tammuz. These antiSemitic sentiments continue to today in virtually all Christian churches. He introduced the messiah of Mithra called Tammuz who became "another Jesus". The stories of Jesus and Tammuz were combined, as were their birthdays. Thus individual Semitic words were replaced with terms of new, anti Semitic meanings comprising Paul's "gospel" events. A representative sample of new, changed terms is: bible, church, Christ, Christian, earth or world, land, law,

Lord, heaven, Old and New Testament, pagan, promised land, rapture, second coming, sojourners, Sunday, Torah, and finally, the one living God, yod hei vav hei. Constantine gave pervasive, official Roman government world wide status to the changes initiated by Shaul earlier with the Roman government's new antiSemitic laws in 70 C.E.. All of this should cause us to realize that we do not have an accurate account of the teachings of Yeshua nor the first century teachings of James and Peter. The 40 years between Jesus' demise and the Temple's demise is a critical period and 100% overlooked by Christendom. They are overlooked because Yeshuaite teachings and practices are left out of Acts.

Nimrod. Long before these two accounts of Constantine's establishment of new religious institutions and the Jupiter worship, a man named Nimrod put together an empire consisting of a one world government with its center in Babylon. It was a political, economic and religious world wide system in which Nimrod was worshiped as God. From the Torah account we know that Nimrod constructed the Tower of *Babel* and that the Almighty crushed his entire operation by giving each of the seventy nations of the earth its own separate language [20]. Nimrod was eventually killed, his body hacked into pieces and scattered throughout the land of Shinar to be eaten by wild animals. One would think that would ensure the end of his story, his government and his religion. Not so. Nimrod's wife, Semiramis sought to retain control of his one world government by declaring that Nimrod had not died but had ascended into the heavens and became the Sun God. One result of the development of this new religion was that the priests of Nimrod divided the year into four quadrants of a solar calendar. Winter solstice is the day of the year with the fewest hours of sunshine or the shortest day of the year; Summer solstice is the longest day of the year measured in minutes of sunlight; The two days of the year with equal amounts of sunlight and darkness in the spring and fall became the vernal and autumnal equinoxi, respectively. This solar calendar of four seasons comprises the pagan origin of the practice of making "the sign of the cross". Sun worshipers touched head then chest and then each shoulder while in turn reciting the names of the four quadrants of the solar calendar. I am saddened to report to you that this is the pagan origin of the sign of the cross. God hates this type of worship.[21]

Semantics: changes in the significance of words over time.

Semiramis. The story of Semiramis continues with enhanced elements of

---

[20] *Linguistic evidence infers that a one world language has existed. The names of the astronomical constellations in some 70 languages today all refer to the same phenomenon for each constellation. E.G. the words for Virgo are the same in Turkish, Chinese, Russian, Hebrew, etc. in that all refer to a virgin.*
[21] *Deuteronomy 11,26 to 28; 12, 1 to 4; 30 and 31. Exodus 20, 1 to3; 23,13.*

sun god legend. It is said she became pregnant and claimed that it had happened via her husband who had impregnated her through the rays of the sun. She produced a son who was proclaimed to be the reincarnated Nimrod. His name was Tammuz and he was born on a day in the ancient Babylonian calendar which corresponds to December 25th. Outside the Vatican in Rome one can today see a statue of Tammuz killing a bull by hand with a knife. Like his father he was a mighty hunter. At age forty, he was gored by a wild boar in a hunting accident. He died. Worshipers of the sun god Nimrod set aside forty days of weeping for him under the theory that if they deny themselves pleasure for forty days in this life, Tammuz will accrue a lifetime of pleasure in his afterlife. Sound familiar? Some time later, Semiramis died.

Easter. It's not over. The sun worship legend is that Semiramis ascended to heaven but the gods sent her back to earth on the first sun day (Sunday) after the vernal equinox. She arrived in Babylon landing in the Euphrates river. She left the water bare breasted as the Goddess of Love (Ishtar). She changed a bird into a rabbit that laid eggs. Thereafter the priests of Easter would assemble before sun rise (Easter Sunrise Service) and impregnate virgins on the altar of Easter. Later the faithful of this religion were urged to sacrifice the babies produced by this religious practice by sacrificing them in a glowing red hot stove (image replicated by Santa's red suit).[22] The blood of these babies was then saved to dye the rabbit eggs of Easter. While all this may sound improbable to the average western gentile Christian, it is common knowledge in the Holy Land. Many residents there are aware of this history and can point you to the places where all this happened. To finish the story: Babylonian sun god priests decreed that the forty days of weeping for Tammuz now became the forty days before the reincarnation of his mother. They implemented the practice of slaughtering a pig as a surrogate of the wild boar which killed Tammuz. They celebrated Easter Sun Day by eating ham. Today in New Orleans, the day before the forty days is celebrated as Fat Tuesday. Many Christians practice the forty days of denial under the title of Lent. So, these are the pagan origins.

Mithra. From the tower of Babel, when Yehovah divided Nimrod's kingdom by scrambling the world's one language into seventy, the worship of Tammuz moved to Persia where it became the worship of Mithra. When Roman soldiers conquered Persia they took on the worship of Mithra which became the Roman sun god *Sol Invictus Mithra*. By the way the Persians were using a unique method of execution for capital crimes: death by crucifiction on a stake. This is one origin of Christianity's adoption of the symbol of the cross. The birthdays of both Tammuz and Mithra were celebrated on the winter solstice: December 25th.

---

[22]*Deuteronomy 12,31.*

(Nowadays the winter solstice physically appears on December 21st.) Both Mithra and Tammuz were portrayed wearing Phrygian caps (the ancestor of Santa's red pointy cap). Two thousand year old coins minted in Rome after Constantine became the first Christian emperor bear the imprint of a man with a crown around the head. He is depicted with the whole world in his hands. It is dated December 25th. Ask anyone nowadays who it is and the likely answer is *that's Jesus*. BUT: The crown is a halo with the rays of the sun coming out of his head. It is a likeness of Constantine. The inscription reads, *"Sol Invictus To Comiti"*. Translation: committed to the invincible sun. Constantine was a worshiper of the sun god Mithra his entire life. He never converted to Christianity.[23] Plenty of such antiquities are misidentified as likenesses of Jesus and so ignorance prevails.

The Cross. The Romans conquered France and they erected the Arch d' Triumph at Orange, years before Jesus lived. The images of the battle standards and shields are portrayed on the arch with a white cross on them. Several hundred years later, the early church fathers wrote their objections to having forced upon them the ancient cross of Mithra which they were being required to use as a symbol for their religion. Constantine was unmoved by their objections and the likeness of a cross became the enduring symbol of Christianity. There is variation in the forms used then to depict the cross.

St. Peter. Today one can see a statue of Saint Peter at Saint Peter's Cathedral in Rome, Italy. It is solid brass. The foot is partially worn away by the kisses of tens of generations of faithful Roman Catholic worshipers. It is the same statue utilized by Antioches Epiphany described at the beginning of this section. Originally a pagan brass statue of Jupiter removed earlier from the Greek pantheon, it came to be deemed holy by church .

So:

He who sacrifices to any god, except to Yehovah only, he shall be utterly destroyed. Exodus 22, 20.

The Culture of the Christian Church

---

[23] *His mother, Helena, whom he dearly loved was a Christian. In fact she drew upon her son the Emperor's resources and liberally preserved many of the church's historical treasure sites. She was the first biblical archeologist and achieved sainthood in the Catholic church. In* **God Hates Religion***, we tend to discount archeology promoted by any given religion. For example two separate Catholic churches buildings claim to have the head of St. Peter.*

As youngsters growing up in Christian society many of us believe in the tooth fairy, the Easter bunny and of course Santa Claus. Usually, prior to entering the teenage years, these beliefs are exposed to the children as harmless cultural fabrications. You may remember shock and mental anguish when you found out that there is no Santa Claus. If so, keep that feeling in mind. Many Americans grow up and perpetuate theses harmless fabrications for their own children so that they can experience the joys of these cultural events. They do bring us good memories of family from the past. In the same way, so do the Hebrew customs of family celebrations of Yehovah's calendered events in the home on Yehovah's holy days. (How good it is to know that one is celebrating one of Yehovah's holy convocations on the same day that He is remembering them). As many Americans mature they go on to live a nominal Christian life in a church or society organized in various ways around these "harmless" holiday events. The fact that these holidays are pagan fabrications is discounted by virtually everyone. This book is describing for you how these fabrications are not harmless. Many of you readers may have preferred to live a reality-based life and only generally abide by cultural ethics rooted in Christianity. You do not claim to live as Christians. A third group we may envision as those who create their own moral rules for living according to what is right in their own eyes. If you are in one of these two latter groups I congratulate you since you are likely to have fewer bad habits to unlearn if you were to investigate the way of Torah. You have not invested in years of following lies from the pagan practices of Christianity. Why would you want to read this book? At some point in everyone's life, as events proceed, all that we have considered to be reality gradually loses its relative importance. We consider that we have found ourselves near the end of our lives and doubts prevail in our thinking. We fantasize about obtaining lasting meaning for ourselves by relating to something larger than ourselves that is worthwhile in its unchangeable truth. We entertain thoughts of God but cannot quite grasp the concept in a form which synchronizes with how we have always truly believed that the truth must be. Let me describe for you two incorrectly applied English terms which have caused millions of people to entertain false ideas about the nature of Yehovah and His words to us: *law* and *lord*.

Law. The Nave's Topical Bible Reference system is time honored by Christian bible scholars the world over. It has several subsections for the word *law*. One subsection is entitled: "Superceded by the Gospel". Nave's organizes its writing around the theory that the Torah of Yehovah has been replaced by the four books detailing the life of Jesus. Ask any Christian, "what is the law?" and they will reference the Ten Commandments. Ask about the Gospel and they will say that Jesus has saved us and set us free from the law. Nave's cites a number of verses to prove their subsection title. One is John 1, 17: **because the Torah was given through**

Moshe and truth and grace through Yeshua the Messiah. For the Christian church this is proof that truth and grace given by Jesus has replaced the Torah of Moshe. You should know that truth and grace do not replace the Torah, rather they fulfill it. What truth and grace do replace however is the condemnation of man made laws from rules developed by religions. Torah does not condemn. It frees. If one looks at the teachings of Jesus there is a pattern to them.[24] He starts with a Torah instruction. *"You have heard that it was said, 'An eye for an eye and a tooth for a tooth'. But I tell you not to resist an evil person. Whoever slaps you on your right cheek, turn the other to him also."*[25] This has become a ubiquitous Christian saying. In many minds it defines a Christian: "Turn the other cheek." However this phrase has an idiomatic meaning in the Aramaic in which it was spoken and written: *Do not start a quarrel or fight.*[26] Jesus did not create a new rule which replaces Torah, rather he was pointing out that there is a blessing to the one who fulfills not only the letter of a torah instruction, but also the spirit of that torah. In so doing the observant one has the Torah of Moshe in his heart. Yeshua is saying it is a blessing to have the Torah written in your heart. **The blessing is a relatively peaceful life**. Fulfilling Torah has it own reward. Christians could embrace the concept of Torah fulfillment, but their religion bypasses Torah. Your pathway to Yehovah leads you also to ***The Hebrew Yeshua V. The Greek Jesus***, by *Nehemiah Gordon*.

Lord. This is a term arising from the 1600s King James English Version of Hebrew and Greek Septuagint sources of Scriptures for Christian bibles. Over the last one thousand years or so any landed gentry in Great Britain have been given the socieo economic status title LORD. Why would the Almighty be given a title as a name. And such a pagan, class ridden British social and economic one at that? *Lord* is tied for first as the poorest translation of a Hebrew term into English in the bible. Abraham acknowledged *El Shaddai* at Hebron and *El Olan* at Beersheba; He paid a tithe to *El Elyon* in Jerusalem; There were local gods to which Abraham gave respect in the days before Yehovah became identified as the Name of the national God of Israel. When the Almighty was ready to reveal His Name to humanity, He spelled it out as **yod, hei, vav, hei** or Yehovah. Most names for God refer to some characteristic that He possesses. They are not what He calls Himself. The first individual to know the actual Name of the Almighty according to Scripture is Moshe. Here in the New King James Version:

---

[24] *Idea from Nehemiah Gordon, a Karaite. See **The Hebrew Yeshua vs the Greek Jesus**. p.61 and ch.10 for a **much** more elegant description.*
[25] *Mattityahu 5, 38 and 39. New King James Version*
[26] *From Proverbs 6, 19. Aramaic was the native language of Jesus. It has a 3,000 year history. It was the native language of the people of Israel from 539 B.C.E. to 70 C.E. It is still spoken by several million people in isolated regions.*

"And God spoke to moses and said to him: 'I am the Lord. I appeared to Abraham, to Isaac, and to Jacob, as God Almighty, but by My name Lord I was not known to them." [27]

My paraphrase: [*He spoke to Moshe and said to him, I am Yehovah. I appeared to Avraham, to Yitz'chak and to Ya'akov, as El Shaddai. But by My Name Yehovah : yod, hei, vav, hei..*יהוה....𐤉𐤄𐤅𐤄... *was I not known to them]*. Contrast this invaluable information with the large number of pagan names that religious churches of the earth have thought up for Yehovah, all borrowed from other local gods. This is just another of so many instances where human traditions have been created out of the mind of man and then MEN have made these created traditions "holy". It is still true today that almost no one on earth proclaims the Name of God. See Ha Shem in chapter 10. Christians and messianics routinely use the word Lord to muddy the distinction between Yehovah and Yeshua, calling them both Lord. This is so imprecise as to be overwhelmingly counterproductive. There is only one Yehovah and He alone is God. In Exodus, 3,13-16 Yehovah states that His Name for all eternity is Yehovah:

Moshe said to God, Look, when I appear before the people of Israel and say to them, The God of your ancestors has sent me to you; and they ask me, What is his name? What am I to tell them? God said to Moshe, " Ehyeh Asher Ehyeh [I am what I am or I will be what I will be]" and He added, " This is what you will say to the people of Israel: Ehyeh has sent me to you." God said further to Moshe, "Say this to the people of Israel: 'yod hei vav hei', Adonai [28] the God of your father, the God of Avraham, the God of Yitz'chak, the God of Ya'akov, has sent me to you. This [Yehovah] is my name forever; this is how I am to be remembered generation after generation."

Forever is a very long time, yet our generation does not use or remember His Name correctly. The religions of our generations do not say His Name: *Yehovah*. And so God hates religion.

Only a few hundred years ago the average educated person living on this planet truly believed that the world was flat. At that time this was common sense, the law of the land and only religious heretics did not believe it. People believed that dragons, sea monsters and fairies of one sort or another were alive in the world and that some of the diverse races of people on the earth were in fact not human. Imagine what kind of thinking the average person believed 3300 years before those times. That was when the Almighty appeared to a man called Avram in the city of Ur of the

---

[27]*Exodus 6, 2 and 3. In my Hebrew bible, the Name in this Scripture is YHWH.*
[28]*Complete Jewish Bible. Note that even David Stern chose to use Adonai as the written expression in lieu of the correct word in the Hebrew Scripture where yod hei vav hei is YHWH , Yehovah or Yahweh in English..*

Chaldees, Babylon. This is the same city of Ur which the United States liberated in southern Iraq only about a decade ago (See Ur, Chapter 10). Abraham was a native Babylonian city dweller. The Almighty appeared to Avram and told him to get out of the city and the land of his ancestors and start traveling to a land that He had in mind for him. By the terebinth tree at Moreh, God appeared to Abraham telling him this land is assigned to your descendants. Abraham moved east of the Canaanite city *Beit El* (lit. House of God). He stayed there, built an altar and invoked the Almighty by name. Thus the beginnings of God's appearances to His people on his land occurred there. Much earlier the Almighty had already caused the letters of His modern Hebrew written Name to appear in the conformation of rocky hills and valleys near the present city of Beit El in the land of Israel. The Christian term is *bethel*. Written in English, these modern Hebrew letters spell yod hei vav hei or Yehovah. The name Yehovah is variously pronounced Yehovah, Yihweh, Yahweh. I have a satellite photograph of the land of Israel hanging on my bedroom wall. The shapes of the letters יהוה are quite evident in the topography of the land of Israel. This is tangible evidence [29]. There is no faith required in order to understand it. Later this book describes other instances of surviving physical evidence. This evidence has come down to us through a time frame exceeding 4,000 years. And it is not only the physical evidence, it is the evidence of the Hebrew Scriptures themselves when each is understood in the context of its language. Many of these archaeological and linguistic facts, as you are seeing, have been hidden from us by millennia of anti Semitism and by various religions which have advocated ignorance of Yehovah's Torah.

Avram was told by the Almighty that he was headed toward a land which his descendants would possess. There they would become a nation of priests of Yehovah called to take His Name to all other peoples of the gentile world. Their mission: proclaim the Name of the Almighty. Ancient Hebrew writings show that one single line of Avram's descendants, Jacob's, witnessed the voice of the Almighty speaking the Ten Words to the nation of Israel on one day. Over the next 40 years additional instructions were given to Moshe for the nation of Israel.

It is important to keep in mind that the Almighty chose the land first and then moved certain descendants of Abraham to it. This is how it is that the nation of Israel came to live in their ancestral homeland, *eretz Israel* or the land of Israel. Yehovah chose that land because that is where He plans to dwell with His people in the future. It is not only the nation of Israel who has a claim on the land. More importantly the

---

[29] *Presently the land is being developed with buildings and* יהוה *being destroyed from the landscape during our lifetimes: Symbolic of man's history.*

Almighty Himself has laid claim to all the land between the Nile river and the Euphrates river. It is true that the culture of the nation of Israel is the only ancient culture surviving intact in that land. None of the other current inhabitants of that land can demonstrate a continuous line of national and cultural identity as can the Israelites. All the other "ites" are gone. However this does not mean that the Almighty has forgotten all other ancient people in the Middle East. In Deuteronomy 2 the Almighty caused the children of (descendants of) Israel to avoid claiming by their footprints several lands that Yehovah had put aside in covenant with other descendants of Abraham not in the lineage of Israel. One was Esau. Israel was not allowed by Yehovah to possess land given to Esau and his descendants. Another is the land of the Moabites who are the descendants of Lot. Yehovah gave Lot his own land. Ruth, of the book of Ruth was a Moabitess. Hebrews generally consider Moabites to be gentiles, however Moshe was buried in the land of the Moabites. See, many scriptural issues transcend BAD v. GOOD. So while Yehovah has laid claim to all the land from the Nile to the Euphrates, this does not mean that it is His plan for Israel to occupy all of His land. Nevertheless, if you look at the description of the Canaanite land given to Israel in Joshua 1,4 it totals about 300,000 square miles! The most Israel has ever actually occupied to date is only about 30,000 square miles. Presently, Israel is a tiny country surrounded by huge nations. Some Day *eretz Israel* will be known to be huge. At that time the nations of the entire world including the United Nations are going to become very interested in the reality of Psalm 24,1 where it says in the **Complete Jewish Bible** version: "**The earth is Adonai's, with all that is in it, the world and those who live there.**" Using the Semitic perspective of the four terms *earth, all, world and live* yields this rendition. Note that it retains the unique literary embellishment of proceeding from the particular to the general case: [*The land of Yisrael is Yehovah's with all the fulfillment of it throughout time; so is the rest of the habitable part of the planet earth and all who dwell there.*]

Yehovah spoke and wrote Torah here on earth at Mount Sinai. His Presence stayed on Mount Sinai for some time. Then His Presence dwelled in the Ark of the Covenant which the nation of Israel carried with them in their forty years following Yehovah's cloud in the desert. Torah says that Mount Sinai is in the land of Midian (Saudi Arabia, not Egypt) and His Presence dwelled upon earth for a total of perhaps half a millennium. In Ezekiel 8 through 11 it is stated that the Presence of Yehovah was observed moving from the Ark to a cherub, above a group of cherubs, to the foundation stones of the temple and then leaving the temple on the temple mount through the East Gate of Jerusalem and ascending the Mount of Olives and disappearing in the sky. This is dated before the second Exile of the people of Israel (586 B.C.E.). Why did He leave? Yehovah refused to dwell in the land of Israel with His chosen people performing acts of pagan religions on His land. Because of their foreign religious activities and failure to let the land rest every seven years, the people of Israel were about to be exiled out of Palestine and into captivity in Babylon. This was the second captivity, the first was in Egypt, *circa* 2,000 B.C.E. King Nebuchadnezzar of Babylon was about to send his conquering army general onto the Temple Mount and into the temple, into the Holy of Holies to capture and bring back to him the world's greatest archeological treasure: THE ARK OF THE COVENANT. The Presence of Yehovah resided in the Ark. Therefore before all this happened, His Presence left the earth. It is Yehovah's stated plan to dwell in the land of Israel living with His people who are observing Torah. We can therefore be sure of one thing: HE IS COMING BACK. So the Good News is that there is a second coming. Most of you have been told that the big event the world is awaiting is the second coming of Christ. Not according to Yehovah's Words. The big event that creation is waiting for is in fact the second coming of Yehovah.... Himself. To sum up then: at Beit El Yehovah had already carved His Name in the rocks on His land where Avram was to go even though that Name was unknown to everyone on the planet. Also the rock letters cannot be seen from any point on the earth and the modern Hebrew script in which it is written had yet to be invented. But as we said, the land was on His Mind.

      These days, except for children taught to believe in the tooth fairy, we do not believe in dragons, sea monsters or fairies. We've seen pictures leading us to believe that the world is a globe in space hurtling through at about 1,000 miles per hour. In addition, our minds are filled with absolutely unimportant garbage facts. From time to time this jingle comes to mind, " *I am stuck on band aids and band aids stuck on me."* Our minds are full of useless facts supporting useless thinking. And while we are on the subject of useless thinking, one of the world's big five religions has some 34,830 culturally distinct denominations.[30] These data demonstrate that we are living in a time of religious nightmare, as if we did not already know from personal experience. Everything is set up to inhibit our ability to zoom in on the truth. It is all diversionary. No one is paying attention to the fact that the Almighty Creator of the Universe physically dwelled here on earth and spoke His Words as an instruction manual for the happy living of human life here on earth. Fewer understand that the events of history, including modern history, are foretold in the nation of Israel's Prophetic Scriptural accounts of their interaction with Yehovah and His plans for the future.

      This book is a shot of rebellion against all this religious chaos. In life there is

---

[30]*Christianity, it is.* David B. Barrett. World Christian Encyclopedia, London: Oxford U. Press, 2001.

already enough drama in the form of catastrophic personal events which occur to otherwise innocent people. Some respond to personal tragedy by seeking to understand the truth about the Almighty. Many respond to their catastrophic event by rejecting the Almighty. Who knows why? One day, when in her mid teens, my oldest daughter asked me, " Dad, why do you believe in God?" A few minutes of silence and I answered *" Because I want to."* The better Scriptural answer to this same question is found succinctly stated in this heavy statement from Jeremiah: **"Thus says [Yehovah]: stand in the ways and see. And ask for the old paths, where the good way is , and walk in it; and you will find rest for your souls. But they said: 'We will not walk in it.'"** [31]

He who sacrifices to any god, except to Yehovah only, he shall be utterly destroyed. Exodus 22, 20.

Yehovah's Torah of Moshe

The ancient fathers such as Noah lived their lives by traveling the old path that they knew led to the Almighty. Their path, the Good Way, is predicated with codes of conduct which predate Yehovah's Torah of Moshe. Torah describes many antediluvian characters (before the Flood), who at some level had friendships with the Creator. Then, in the times of Noah long before people had any written knowledge of Yehovah, Scriptures tell us that every man was doing what was right in his own eyes. This paganism resulted in so much evil upon the earth that Yehovah totally destroyed it with The Flood. We should look upon Torah then as God's provision to keep man from again perverting the entire world down the toilet of evil living practices. Torah in this light should be understood by western gentile believers as Yehovah's big Plan of salvation for mankind. Its goal is a total end to evil in the world. But with Yehovah there is not even a shadow of turning [change]. So also His words remain unchanged. If you decide this subject is the only one worthy of your lifelong attention you should be aware that even with your best efforts there is far too much information out there to be studied in one lifetime. Hundreds of thousands, maybe millions of learned Torah observant men in thousands of highly disciplined schools through the ages have labored their whole lives to understand the complete story of Torah. This search has been going on for a very long time and it continues. We should have some appreciation for the puny part gentiles play in the history of mankind's search for Yehovah Himself.

Our attempts to understand what was in Yehovah's speeches involve several

---

[31] *Jeremiah 6,16. The New King James Version paraphrased with one word: The Name Yehovah.*

issues. One is getting a true English translation of the Torah, and Tanakh. Secondly we would like a Torah based English translation of the Aramaic scriptures known today as the Christian New Testament (NT). If you are relatively young, there would be a payoff in learning Hebrew and Aramaic. If any of you long to be part of an organized religion, you may examine the need to join Judaism. Think like a Karaite. You should know that if you had been born into an observant Jewish family as a male child, you would have had to have memorized the entire five scrolls of Torah by about age twenty. So do not dismiss lightly the understanding of the Jewish people as they are quite far ahead of all of us western gentiles. One should also not dismiss lightly the Jewish people who in pagan western gentile minds seem to be atheists. As citizens of the nation of Israel they are very familiar with Torah as it is both their national Constitution *and* the history of their ancestors.

In Tanakh we find the Writings and the Prophets. These writings consist of history such as Chronicles as well as poetic writings such as Psalms. They recount the human history of Yehovah's interaction with people on earth. They are historical commentary on Torah. Real action is in the Prophets writings of the Tanakh. While prophetic scrolls are not part of the most revered Scriptures, Torah, they carry weight because the prophets spoke as the mouthpiece of Yehovah. How did the Hebrews determine that a self proclaimed prophet was in fact speaking as the mouthpiece of God? They didn't. Their scribes wrote down everything he said. After a few years they usually got tired of all the prophetic ranting and executed the individual. Years, even generations later when a prophet's prophecies began coming true, the Sanhedrin would realize they had killed one of the Yehovah's prophets. Lest you think ill of the Sanhedrin, realize they were carrying out the Torah's charge to rule Israel without changing Torah, upon pain of death. Because scribes wrote down every word spoken before the Sanhedrin by that prophet, the written record of the deceased prophets became the scrolls of Isaiah, Jeremiah Ezekial, Zechariah, etc after the prophecies were validated in history. There it is again: **Prophecy becoming history**. There is no scroll of Yeshua. What happened? Highjacking of his prophetic role?

From the scrolls of these prophets we can learn where we stand on Yehovah's time line of future events. They give us a glimpse of what some modern global events mean and where life on earth is headed. We all have to avoid the pitfalls of false witnesses. A false witness refers not to perjury in a trial, but to those who change Yehovah's words in Torah and then communicate these falsified changes as truth to others. See, the Christian church has the same dilemma that occupied the Sanhedrin. Personally, I do not wish to falsely witness Yehovah to my own children nor to you in writing **God Hates Religion**. Therefore, know that His Plan for His land and His people has not changed. We generate false witness of Him if we say that the Old Testament (Torah) has been replaced by the NT. This alludes to a lurking issue in what it is that the Almighty has told us. That is *interpretation*.

The Almighty is aware that humans have the propensity to prevaricate, but He speaks of a time when His children will surely not lie. In giving us Torah, there are a number of safeguards built in to discourage tampering with it in any way. The Almighty knew that many generations of men would try to change His words. In this book you will read at some length about methods men have historically used to change His words. They can all be described with one commonality and that is by employing substitute terms which have vague meanings. A two bit English label for that kind of fuzzy subterfuge is **terminological inexactitude**. In America we have for centuries been given English "translations" of the Torah which change all the names of the people and many key word concepts including the very word Torah itself. The Torah (consisting of physical objects, i.e. scrolls of ancient writings) has been changed to The Law (a mental concept which is the vaguest of the vague and the broadest of the broad). It is so broad a term that it can be used to refer to almost anything. It is an inexact term. It has a meaning for gentile Americans which is vastly different from the meaning of the ancient writings in Torah. As a result of these types of stumbling blocks to the ancient truths we have all inherited inexactitudes in what we have been told about the Almighty and Scripture.[32] These are lies then and they are pervasive but subtle. There are prophetic scriptures predicting that it would happen this way. We need all the Semitic language and culture left in our translations of Scripture. Otherwise we get the several levels of compounded misunderstandings in the minds of all parties. This is easily demonstrated by this simple domestic interaction:

A little girl goes up to her mother who is washing dishes in the kitchen sink. *"You're the tooth fairy, aren't you Mom?"* she asks. With a sigh her mother replies that she is (meaning "Yes, I have been giving you money under the pillow for your lost teeth"). But then the girl asks: "Can I see the dress?" This is an example of two generations using the same words, yet their thoughts are far apart.

With one exception, all religions and cultural systems of ethics and morality have been created by the minds of a very small group of people or even only one man: Nimrod, Constantine, Alexander the Great, Hitler. These are all classic cases of religious or moral systems used in historical attempts to dominate the world by enslaving the minds of the people of this earth. There is only one instance where a religious or moral system has appeared to us from outside the realm of human

---

[32] *Jeremiah 16, 19 to 21. In Hebrew the last word in this quote is yod hei vav hei or YHWH, not Lord.*

imagination. *One time* that such a system has been conceived in the presence of such a great cloud of witnesses as an entire nation of two million people. Read the account of the Torah events at Mt. Sinai in both Exodus and Deuteronomy in a good English translation, such as by the Jewish Publication Society. The best is a translation where facts are not lost due to a story form rendition of the events.

Here is an example of story form. In Genesis 32 19 to 21 we find a tale of Jacob and Esau. It is the first time that Jacob has seen his brother Esau in years since he tricked Esau out of their father's inheritance, the family land. Jacob sends messengers to Esau to tell him that he is coming to him for a visit. The messenger comes back to Jacob with the electrifying news that Esau is right behind him and he is coming with 400 armed warriors! Jacob is in mortal fear of the danger to his life and he concocts a solution that he hopes will save his life. He sends a present to Esau and tells his emissaries, here it is in the New King James: **"In this manner you shall speak to Essau when you find him; and also say, 'Behold your servant Jacob is behind us.' For he said, 'I will appease him with the present that goes before me, and afterward I will see his face; perhaps he will accept me.' So the present went on over before him, but he himself lodged that night in camp."** That is a story rendition of the events. It might as well have been written by the Associated Press (AP). It doesn't really tell you what is going on with Jacob's plan to save himself with a gift. From Everett Fox this English translation uses a rendition of the sequence of events which is true to the Torah's embellishments. It describes Jacob's thinking using the play of the sounds in Hebrew [33] of variations in the recurring word PANIM, which means *face*.

> **"For he said to himself:**
> **I will wipe (the anger from) his face (phanav)**
> **with the gift that goes ahead of my face, (le phanai)**
> **Afterwards, when I see his face, (phanav)**
> **Perhaps he will lift up my face (phanai)**
> **The gift crossed over ahead of his face (al panav).**[34]

Aside from the elegant beauty of this aural translation, there is a key factor here that is elaborated rather than being minimized. Our thinking is pointed to the theme of face. A face is not a concept. It is a concrete thing. We always strive to go back from some general concept some English translation dangles in front of us to

---

[33] *YHWH ordered that the Torah be read aloud to the people and also sung to them. Hence sound is important for authenticity. The characters of written Hebrew are symbols of the spoken consonants of speech.*
[34] *Genesis 32, 21 and 22. Everett Fox, **The five Books of Moses**, pp. xi and 153, 155.*

the actual concrete phrases that the Hebrew Scriptures contain. This is how we proceed in our quest to avoid religious generalities in our pursuit of the exact Words from the Almighty.

It also happens that the word face provides a cue for the next big event described at the end of Genesis 32. We would have missed it if we had not been given the mindset of face. Jacob is left alone and wrestles with a Man. Neither submitted the other. Jacob requested a truce in the form of a blessing from the Man. The Man gave Jacob a new name to commemorate this event: Israel. He is told he will be called Israel because he struggled with God and with man and has prevailed. Jacob called that place "Peniel" (does that sound familiar?) because he had seen the Face of God and lived to tell about it. This episode in the Torah is important for us to understand because: 1). Some current occupants of Jerusalem, Palestine and most of the Promised Land from the Nile river to the Euphrates river may be descendants of Essau and Lot and have the right to be in their part of the land. With these few exceptions all other foreign faces belong to Torahless peoples who do not belong there. That they should be living there on Yehovah"s land is not in His plan; 2). The concept of face is ubiquitous. Even a cup of coffee has a face in Middle Eastern culture, if it is a correctly brewed cup (a Hebrew):) 3). The nation of Israel has struggled with God and with man and has prevailed. They still face us some three thousand years later; 4) It is not true that Yehovah has forsaken Israel in these present times. He has only temporarily turned His Face from them [35]; 5) The Almighty tells us that in the future He will redeem His people with the " messenger of His Face"; and finally this event signifies the first time appearance of the One God of the nation of Israel on the ground here on earth in the land of Canaan. And thus some of us are led to the dual conclusions that the hope for the future is in Messiah and Messiah is a messenger of the Face of God. All of this because someone took the time to correctly elevate an operative term, face, in the translation into English. Now if the word face can this easily be shown to have this level of importance that we should have it straight in our minds, don't you think that it is even more important to use the correct **name** for the Almighty? That way we will be able to distinguish between the Almighty and His messengers such as Yeshua. Yet Christian thinking, writing and talking routinely refers to both God and Jesus as Lord. Supreme terminological inexactitude.

The nation of Israel is the witnesses to Torah.[36] **They are the faces of Torah.** The benefit they receive is promised to the nation's father, Abraham in

---

[35] *Deuteronomy 32, 20. He promised He would hide His face.*
[36] *Isaiah 43,10.*

Genesis 12, 3. The Almighty promises to bless anyone blessing Abraham's chosen descendants and that He will curse anyone who curses Abraham's descendants. He promised that in Abraham's family shall all the families of the earth be blessed. Yehovah says that this promise shall be for all time. This means that no terms of the promise can be replaced with new terms. Most foreign nations have historically been jealous of God's choice of Israel to receive His special blessings. Despite the determined effort of literally hundreds of nations to exterminate all this Hebrew witness from the face of the earth, the Israelites have endured and even thrived. Their continued existence is compelling evidence to the truth of their relationship with Yehovah. As Mark Twain said when he was asked why he believed in God: *The Jews, the Jews. They are the only ancient peoples left. All the other "ites" are extinct.* Moreover, we point out that their languages are also extinct: Phoenician, Ammonite, Moabite, Edomite *et.al.*. Yet Hebrew thrives.

In contrast to the plans of the Almighty, human thought changes. Anything human beings can control they begin changing. They fiddle with it. There are a few things we have not been able to change: earthquakes, the weather, asteroid impacts. Most importantly man has not been able to obliterate either Yehovah's Torah nor the descendants of the man Israel.

Because of the way in which it has been constructed by the Almighty and the way it has been brought down to us through the ages, we have good reasons to believe the Torah is authentic. All Kings of Israel were required to make their own copy of the Torah, a task otherwise done by the scribes. King Solomon took it upon himself to alter a single word with one tiny stroke. The Torah instructs everyone that no changes to it are allowed: no additions, no subtractions. Solomon paid for this disobedience. While all of Israel is aware of the prohibition against any changes whatsoever to Torah, few if any gentiles realize its importance. Either that or they are cynical. The point is that no one, not even Jesus can change Torah. In Matthew 5, 17 to19, Jesus said in the *Complete Jewish Bible*:

"Don't think that I have come to abolish the Torah or the Prophets. I have come not to abolish but to complete. Yes indeed! I tell you that until heaven and earth pass away, not so much as a yud or a stroke will pass from the Torah...not until everything that must happen has happened. So whoever disobeys the least of the mitzvot [individual instructions or torahs] and teaches others to do so will be called the least in the Kingdom of Heaven. But whoever obeys them and so teaches will be called great in the Kingdom of Heaven".

Ironically this statement of Yeshua was the **first** thing that anti Semitic leaders changed in the construction of a new gospel story of Jesus meant for the gentiles. Shaul or other Torah breakers claimed that Yeshua had replaced the Torah with new commandments. Wrong, Yeshua lived his life on a mission fulfilling

Torah. The essential fact is that Yeshua died defending Torah. The Christian church bible is descended however from Greek Septuagint translations of Tanakh. (It was the first Greek version of Torah written by 72 learned Hebrew elders at the bidding of the Hellenistic ruler of Egypt, Ptolemy II.) Its NT versions are not sourced direct from its Aramaic writings, nor from the Torah doctrines of James, Peter and the Yeshuaites. The NT savages Torah; Not only changes it but renders it null and void, replaced by Jesus the Messiah. So we see twisting of the Words of Yehovah, the original, unchangeable standard of truth.

What of the Christian teaching that Jesus is the only Savior? Yehovah says: **"Besides Me there is no savior"** (Isaiah 43, 11). And in Matthew 15, 21 to 24, in the words of the NT, Jesus speaks against the idea he is the gentile savior. **He who sacrifices to any god, except to Yehovah only, he shall be utterly destroyed. Exodus 22, 20.**

LAND : An Overlooked Factor

The Tanakh frequently references the various peoples of the earth not by their names but by the name of the land wherein they dwell. The land of Shinar, the land of Goshen and the land of Egypt are but a few. When it comes to *eretz Israel*, the land of Israel, Yehovah has claimed his ownership of all the land from the Nile river to the Euphrates and from the Mediterranean Sea to as far east as the thirteen tribes walked upon in their forty years following Yehovah's cloud to the land of the Canaanites. As we have pointed out, they have to date occupied only about 30,000 square miles out of the 300,000 which Yehovah has set aside for them.

In the Torah, many of the instructions are in regard to tithes, offerings and sacrifices that are associated with the Feasts of Yehovah and with priestly temple events and individuals seeking forgiveness. The Passover Sacrifice may not be what you think: the operation of this sacrifice is that the people are to eat the sacrifice as a feast [37]! The *animal* is sacrificed, Yehovah's people benefit! A second surprise: the source of all the produce used in tithes, offerings and sacrifices IS the land of Israel. There is no provision for a Torah observant person to make these from the produce of other lands! The land of Israel is very special. [38] Torah instructs us that we give thanks to Yehovah AFTER one has eaten and is full and the point is that thanks is given for the good land Yehovah has given us. Yehovah has a rather famous

---

[37] *Leviticus 19, 6 to 8; and 14, 22 to 26.*
[38] *Deut. 12, 11. God cares for your promised land. His eyes are on it every day of the year from the first day to the last day of the year.*

provision for letting the land REST. If the seventh day of the week is a day of rest from labor for human beings, then the seventh year is a year of rest for Eretz Israel wherein the land rests from its labor to provide agricultural produce or food. Israel's second captivity in Babylon was caused by violating this 7th year of rest for Eretz Israel. In ancient times there was often not enough food for everyone to eat until full. Cows were much smaller and were treasured as symbols of wealth. Perishable meat was mostly eaten on special occasions, hence meat was only eaten when a feast was appropriate. Food scarcities combined to cause ancient peoples to routinely consume iffy food presumably with the usual negative results. On those rare days when one had eaten enough to be full it was appropriate to give thanks to Yehovah for the good land. It was at that time considered to be a lack of trust in God to pray first and then eat. Yet the Christian church universally maintains a tradition of saying "grace" before all meals. Yehovah gave us instructions in which the land was emphasized over the food and thanks was given after one is full rather than before the meal. In Deuteronomy 8, 10 Yehovah directs His people:

"When you have eaten and are full, then you shall bless the Lord your God for the good land which He has given you."

Ignoring this direct and simple torah from Yehovah is a common Torahless practice of religious peoples who give thanks before the meal. Undoubtedly most forget to mention the land. Any nation which dismisses Israel and their Torah observant cultural practices and then claims to be their replacement for the blessings of Yehovah violates Yahoveh's Words. They poke a finger in God's Eye.[39]

He who sacrifices to any god, except to Yehovah only, he shall be utterly destroyed. Exodus 22, 20.

The Jerusalem Temple, *Yehovah's* Sanctuary

Ezekial 8, 6 tells us that abominations occurring at Yehovah's Temple caused His Holiness Yehovah to distance Himself from His own sanctuary.[40] If you were to stop and read Ezekial 8 and 9 right now, you will notice that in Ezekial's vision, Yehovah grabbed Ezekial by the hair of his head and forced him to look at three abominations occurring in the Temple and throughout Jerusalem. Both 8, 16 and 11, 1 to 4 describe the same 25 men of Jerusalem worshiping the sun. What is the name

---

[39] *Zechariah 2, 8.*
[40] *2 Chronicles 30, 13 to 27. God is holy. Anyone who eats Passover meal without first purifying incurs the death penalty. God is holy, but men travel out of town, contract an unclean illness, etc. and are unable to get temple purification. God is holy, men are not. He would have to kill everyone, but Hezekiah, the man of God prayed for forgiveness for everyone. God had mercy.*

of the day of the week that the Christian church chooses to worship the Almighty? What is the day of the week in which you personally worship God? In Ezekial, pagan practices performed on the Temple Mount and at the Temple in Yehovah's presence had a very bad consequence. A mark (the letter tav ~ X) was placed on the forehead of every person in Jerusalem observed to be wailing in lament of the abominations being committed in Jerusalem.[41] Everyone else was killed. Then Yehovah left the earth. What will He find when He returns to this earth? Ironically, the same 25 X men had only turned to sun worship because everyone else in Jerusalem had already been destroyed and these 25 had lost all hope. They believed they were next. Lest you incorrectly harbor any anti Semitic thoughts about this situation, consider Ezekial 14, 7 wherein strangers living in Jerusalem also "broke from Me" to consult diviners and other false prophets in the land. Christian churches physically present in Jerusalem today continue to perform pagan acts in Jerusalem and in the land of Israel all the time thinking they are doing God's work. It continues to this day. If Yehovah did not spare these Hebrew Jerusalemites, His oldest friends on the earth, why would He spare modern day stranger abominators? In the light of what we have just discussed from Ezekial 8 and 9 is there anything more important to organize one's time around than the wailing wall in Jerusalem? **Yehovah, He, watching over Israel.** Some day the scene described by Ezekial 8 and 9 may be repeated but on the grand scale. Bluntly, we need to recognize this is our present day situation. We should pray for peace in Jerusalem by lamenting the pagan practices on His holy land. *God Hates Religion* proposes that we pray for an end to all foreign religions in Jerusalem. That is a concrete way to pray for peace in Jerusalem. **All elements of sun worship must vanish before Yehovah returns.**

In this chapter we have demonstrated in His words Yehovah's thinking about His Name, the role of face, the House of God, the words of God and the land of God. We have explored these elements: The Name Yehovah, His thinking and actions about ancient pagan practices near His sanctuary in the city of Jerusalem, American cultural Christianity, the Torah and the land of Israel. In Ezekial 8 through about 14 you were reminded that Yehovah has already created a plan to cleanse His land of both Hebrews and Sojourners who turn from His Torah and embrace foreign, pagan worship practices. From the human standpoint Yehovah's cleansing plan will be violent. Zechariah 5,1 assures nuclear war in Israel.

The teachings of the Christian church prefer to have their followers believe

---

[41] *First century archaeological findings show that the Jesus is Messiah movement adopted this symbol as their own. It appears on ossuaries (bone boxes) and in the Galilean town of Bethsaida where first century dwellings are still at ground level.*

that the "Law", Torah is impossible for anyone to observe and that is why we need Jesus to be our Savior. Those teachings challenge Yehovah, Who said in clear words: 1) the Torah lifestyle I have given you today is not too hard for you, it is NOT beyond your reach; 2) There is no Savior but Me (Isaiah 43,11); 3) I share My glory with no one (Isaiah 42,8). And so we say that Yehovah hates (turns His Face from) religion.

Chapter 4

Princes of This World

Machiavelli wrote a book called *The Prince* which advises people of authority how to gain and keep power. For rulers of peoples, governments and corporations the number one goal is survival. This goal transcends any other moral, ethical or religious value including the well being of any people subject to their power. *Princes of this world* is alluded to in Ephesians 6, 12 in the Ancient Eastern Manuscript's description of a phenomenon which says:

"For your conflict is not only with flesh and blood, but also with angels, and with powers, with the rulers of this world of darkness (princes), and with the evil spirits under the heavens."

History describes various persons who are human appointed messiahs, called divine or holy only by humans and not so appointed by Yehovah: Nimrod, Tammuz, Constantine, Adolf Hitler, Emperor Hirohito, the Pope. Nowadays we find ourselves living in exciting times when dormant ancient Semitic knowledge is again being honored. The Jewish people are returning from many nations to their ancestral homeland of Israel. Certain preparations to restart the Jerusalem temple signal the approaching fulfillment of prophecy. While many are not so inclined, at least one Torah observant Jew, Nehemiah Gordon, is teaching gentiles the true Hebraic meanings of biblical terms.

The first named person in history to qualify as a Prince of this world was a man named Nimrod. He conquered the known world and ruled it with a one world linguistic, religious and economic government. Satan's description to Eve about the effects of eating the forbidden fruit had come true as Nimrod was well on his way to becoming Like God. Nimrod's run on God produced two legacies for the human race that continue to this day. The Almighty shut Nimrod's operation down by changing the one language, Hebrew, spoken by all the peoples of the earth to seventy languages: one for each nation. This halted Nimrod's construction of the Tower of Bavel and ended Nimrod's one world government. Today the intellectual elite of many nations, who are those most likely to benefit from it, still dream and plan for a new one world government. The plan already exists. It is called Torah. It does have for the elite the disadvantage that Yehovah Himself runs it. After his passing from the earth, Nimrod's wife claimed she had ascended to the Sun and come back to earth, splashed down in the Euphrates river reincarnated as the Sun God Mithra and rose up bare breasted as Ishtar the goddess of fertility. She place her son Tammuz in charge of the government as the reincarnated Nimrod produced by her union with the sun. The effects of sun god worship are still with us today and both Christianity and even Judaism have been affected by it (there is a Jewish month named Tammuz). With all this talk about the sun, we should realize that Yehovah has His own ideas about the role of the sun. Deuteronomy 4,19 says **[Do not worship the sun, moon or the stars.]**

Concerning Tammuz, we go to Ezekial 8, 14 and 15 in the New King James:

"So He brought me to the door of the north gate of the Lord's house: and to my dismay, women were sitting here weeping for Tammuz. Then He said to me: Have you seen this, O son of man? Turn again, you will see greater abominations than these."

First let us notice that the Almighty called His prophet Ezekial "son of man". This is how Yehovah referred to His prophets, his messengers. Coincidentally, this is also how Jesus referred to himself: son of man. These women are weeping for Tammuz who in his fortieth year of life was gored to death by a wild boar. Today many Christians observe forty days of Lent. It celebrates one day for each year of Tammuz' life. This observance culminates in the western gentile religious celebration of Easter (Ishtar) SUN day by the consumption of a meal of baked ham. *Triple breaking of Torah*. In the traditional Judaic calendar the 4th month which overlaps the western months of June and July is named Tammuz. Some day Yehovah will excise all pagan names. (Hosea 2, 18 and 19).

Let me give you just three example from among hundreds, maybe thousands, that demonstrate pagan roots in many old institutions, even in the Roman Catholic church. 1) In St. Peter's Basilica, the Sistine chapel has a statue of St. Peter. The foot is worn away from two thousand years of kisses from the lips of the faithful.

Sad to say, the statute was not created as a representation of Peter, the apostle. It has no Christian origin at all. It is a pagan statute passed off as a sacred object by the Roman church which obtained it as an archaeological artifact originating in the Greek Pantheon. It was created as a likeness of the pagan god Jupiter; 2) The tall hat worn by the Pontiff was borrowed directly from the hats worn by worshipers of the Egyptian fish god Dagon. These hats are replicas of a fish with its open mouth pointing upward. This is the same Dagon who was found to be powerless to rule over the fish or the waters of the Nile river. You may recall the many miracles Moses performed culminating in the repetitious command for Pharaoh to "Let my people go". Moses turned the waters of the Nile to blood red which killed all the fish throughout the river. This demonstrated Dagon's impotence as a god. Each of Moses' miracles was done in such a way as to demonstrate the inability of each Egyptian god to have any effect whatsoever in their respective domains. Why would anyone who believes the ancient story of deliverance from Pharaoh by Yehovah incorporate such a pagan practice into their relationship with Yehovah? 3) Almost all the religious artifacts, customs and even the very exalted names church officials applied to the Pontiff, e.g. "THE HOLY SEE" are borrowed from the many ancient pagan religions existing in Egypt, Greece, Babylon and Assyria. Troubling, isn't it?

Today millions of western gentile Christian churches observe the Sabbath not on the seventh day of the week, but the next day, on the first day of the week. Can it please the Almighty that they are resting and then working instead of working and then resting? In the creation account it is written that God's practice of resting on the seventh day after six days of work is meant for us human beings to be a holy blessing. God blessed the seventh day and called it holy. The next time you consider, "Be holy, even as I am Holy", recall resting on the Sabbath day, the sign of keeping Torah.

In the fourth century CE the emperor Constantine successively outlawed all things Jewish, Hebrew and Torah from his new empire wide religion which he designated Christianity. He made the exercise of all Jewish traditions capital crimes. It was Constantine who changed the Sabbath to the first day of the week. It had absolutely nothing to do with the resurrection of Yeshua. Up until that day it had been a capital crime to practice Christianity. Overnight Christianity became the official state religion of his newly expanded empire. It suddenly became a capital crime *not* to be a Christian. In spite of this, Constantine himself was a devout worshiper of the sun god *sol Invictus Mithra* for his entire life to the day he died. He made the above changes only to unify all the religions in his empire making it easier to govern. He was only running a big organization. Nowadays, the Pope runs a big organization. THIS IS HOW A PRINCE OF THIS WORLD OPERATES. Constantine was a Torahless pagan all his life. In spite of this reality, if you ask Christians why they insist on calling the first day of the week the Sabbath, they usually answer it is out of respect for Jesus who arose from the dead on the first Easter Sunday. He did? Aside from the lack of historical authenticity, consider Yeshua's words from Matthew 12, 39 to 40 from the New King James:

"..An evil and adulterous generation seeks after a sign, and no sign will be given it except the sign of the prophet Jonah. For as Jonah was three days and three nights in the belly of the great fish, so will the Son of Man be three days and three nights in the heart of the earth."

As many have noted, from Good Friday to Easter Sunday is not three days and three nights. And so Christianity has continued the pagan religious practices of sun god worship and in so doing is a part of the evil and (Torahless) generation referred to by Yeshua. Again, God hates religion. However, *some day* a man of God may intervene to pray for their forgiveness.

Chapter 5

The Name God Calls Himself

Today, everything a person in the western world is likely to know about the Creator of the Universe comes from various interactions with a western religion. The origin, the prime source of all western religion's information is Torah of Moshe. It is still in use, unaltered, by the same nation of Middle Eastern tribes to whom it was given. While some westerners may have Hebrew family roots, few gentiles actually know Torah. It is a new beginning then, to totally dismiss every false thing we learned about the Hebrew's God from our western culture. As foreign ideas intervening from organized religion disappear from one's mind, we can become acquainted with the Almighty and with His Words on His basis. It starts with the fact that at last we foreigners know His Name: *Yehovah;* ;יהוי;. ⲯⲨⲯⳮ· pronounced *Yehovah, Yahweh* or *Yihweh* (except by many observant Jewish persons who express it as *Adonai* or *Ha Shem, The Name*). The three patriarchs of biblical faith: Avram, Yitz'chak and Ya'akov all did not know God by this Name *yod, hei, vav, hei* for their entire lives. The first person in Scriptures to know what the Almighty calls Himself is Moshe. See Exodus 6, 3. Everyone who writes a new translation of the bible or a book on a biblical theme very quickly finds the need to explain the names of God. It's a ridiculous situation. The many names for God are all words we westerners or other foreigners use to describe some character trait of God. They are not what God Himself calls Himself. They are not God's NAME. Here's the background: When Moshe carried Yehovah's message to Pharaoh, **"Let my people go"**, the reply was always the same, "No, I am Pharaoh." His negative reply to Moshe always ended with his statement of authority: *I am Pharaoh.* In the end, Yehovah put his Signature on the issue of final authority when Moshe, speaking as the mouthpiece of God, told Pharaoh: **"Let My people go, I am Yehovah."** The point is that this episode is the first revelation of the Almighty's Name Yehovah to a human being. However a casual reading of Torah from its beginning does not reveal the fact that Moshe was the first to know. The ancient author, presumed to be Moshe, *retroactively* inserted the word *yod, hei, vav, hei*: 𐤉𐤄𐤅𐤄 in the paleo form, into his interactions with the Almighty that occurred before he knew the Name Yehovah. Alternatively, in Torah passages before Exodus 6, 3 subsequent copiers, writers, translators and possibly editors of Scripture, (if there were any) and translations liberally replaced the ancient Hebrew forms of Yehovah: 𐤉𐤄𐤅𐤄, יהוה with other names such as *El, El Shaddai, HaShem, Lord* or *Adonai*. So in Scriptures written before the actual revelation to Moshe, the Almighty's Name likely was backwritten as Yehovah. A third explanation is that Exodus 6, 3 rhetorically means to say the following thought: "By my name, Yehovah, was I not known to them? Of course not. They did not know My Name." In these early eras of the Torah episodes, Yehovah was known to these ancestor Patriarchs and their related Canaanite tribes by local names such as *L, El, El Shaddai*. Torah throughout demonstrates the Hebrew Patriarchs and some of the Canaanites all knew the same Creator, in fact *Yehovah*. Later, by 1800 B.C.E., there is evidence that some Canaanites possessed a proto Sinaitic or Proto Hebraic written pictographic symbol for the Creator: 𐤋 . English translators, acting 3,000 years later with supreme terminological inexactitude chose to provide words they felt had equivalent meanings. There is no equivalent meaning for the Name Yehovah. While neither Judaism nor Christianity historically have reported His Name accurately, for Israel no judgement is intended here. How could I, I am not a rabbi.[42] We foreigners are ignorant: Jewish Scriptural dilemmas are largely unknown to us.

    Christianity's failure to report His Name accurately however, has no Scriptural basis. For a thousand years in the British Isles landowning gentry have been called "Lord". To emphasize the Almighty's stature rising above low class masses, the King James version began referring to Yehovah as Lord. In truth, they were ignorant of Hebrew and could not decipher the Hebrew characters of His Name, which appeared to them the word *pipi*. Adding to the confusion of calling the Almighty by the socioeconomic term *Lord*, the Christian church's writings also refer to Jesus by the word *Lord*. At any given time it is impossible to tell if a Christian is referring to Yehovah or to Jesus. Supreme terminological inexactitude.

---

[42] *Who am I that I should tell Yahweh that I do not approve of the way He has handled His servant Israel or that his servant Israel has not served Him well?*

In contrast, Judaism has a Torah based rationale for their actions. It is inferred that the Name is too sacred to casually pass through the lips of a human being, and what is written can be destroyed or even read aloud. Therefore we see the word G*d. They have other reasons. We read startling biblical sentences such as Genesis 1,1: **[In the beginning, the name created heaven and earth.]** Many believe that this rule against expressing The Name came about as a result of the Rabbis attempting to ensure compliance with the third commandment: **"You shall not take the name of Lord your God (Yehovah) in vain (lightly), for the Lord will not hold him guiltless who takes His name in vain."** However this third commandment refers solely to the issue of oath taking, **not cursing**. You shall not swear *falsely* in the Name of Yehovah, *by My Name*. In vain, represents the falsehood of swearing on God's Name that something is true, all the time knowing it is false. It happens in court rooms all the time. **FYI, this is the unforgivable sin**. Indeed, the Aramaic of the Eastern Peshitta says to not take a false oath in the name of your God (Exodus, 20, 7). The bottom line is that Hebrews have understood another torah, Deuteronomy 12, 3 and 4 to prohibit the destruction of His Name. Well, if it gets written down, it can be destroyed.[43] There is a beauty to this detailed thinking that makes westerners look like bulls in a china closet. The issue is created by two apparently contradictory torahs (little t meaning an individual instruction, a single point). Yehovah knows the truth, we do not. If nothing else it shows the moral courage of the Jewish mindset to attempt to keep ALL Torah. Scripture shows that Yehovah's goal is for the Jewish people to be His witnesses to all the nations on the earth. They were given the job of being earthly witnesses of His Name Yehovah. The irony remains. How can one witness the Almighty's Name if one is discouraged from saying aloud or writing that word? How would any of *us* know what His Name is? The bottom lines is that it is best for foreigners not to be impatient with, nor to criticize Yehovah's witnesses.

    The Christian church has Torahlessly chosen to say or write Lord in place of Yehovah. They have no scriptural basis for failing to fulfill their self induced command for themselves to witness His Name. So, which name would they be witnessing? The timing for how this issue plays out in the future is up to Yehovah. Know that if you were to find a rabbi and convince him to give you a blessing, he would likely tell you to humble yourself (assume a humble posture) and ask HaShem aloud three times to help you, then he say the prayer. You would realize that the

---

[43] *If one Google Earths Beit El, Israel, in the area of 31deg 54 min 23.15 sec N by 35d 13m 54.44m E at 846 meters elevation, construction in the area is destroying the contours of the land which spell out His Name* יהוה.

rabbi truly has a personal link to approach HaShem. You would understand and go away *glowing*. **Christians do not own the spirit of God**.

Churches should give up praying, *in Jesus name* when it is realized once and for all that His Name is not Jesus. His Name is Yehovah and He is the object of all prayer. **[Blessed is he who comes in the Name of Yehovah]**. You may be thinking, well I am covered under grace. So if I call Him Jesus, God will cut me some slack. Consider this: Grace and truth atone for iniquity, Proverbs 16, 6a, recalling that iniquity refers to living without Torah. You are claiming grace not knowing that it refers to something else, a personal behavior of the Almighty. Praying in Jesus' name is a human tradition that men have themselves labeled holy. It kills the heart of Yeshua's monotheistic teachings and his three times daily recitation of Sh'ma (God is One). Jesus was a monotheist who never personally claimed to be divine.

Secondly, the Hebrews have received more mercy via grace than any other people who have ever existed. They are His oldest friends on earth (Isaiah chapter 43). They are the apple of His eye. They enjoy a unique protection guaranteed for all time by Yehovah (Genesis 12, 3). Have they been successful in obtaining God's grace in order to avoid experiencing penalties built into disobedience of the Torah? Of course they haven't. In the Song of Moshe in Deuteronomy 32 the Almighty tells of a plan to use gentile believers to carry His Name to the nations of the earth on a temporary basis. The purpose for employing gentiles for this work is solely to evoke jealousy among the Hebrews. See you can communicate by carrier pigeon but eventually it becomes so inefficient that it loses its utility. The gentile mission is more temporary than they realize.

God has Written His Name In Big Letters

As previously noted, on our bedroom wall, there is mounted a large satellite photograph of the land of Israel with modern geographical boundaries. About twenty kilometers north of Jerusalem is a town called *Beit'el*. *Beit* = house; *'el* = God. Directly below the site is a row of mountain ridges in shadow relief. Written in modern Hebrew symbols the mountain says **yod hei vav hei**, reading from the right: י ה ו ה to left. On the mountain it is south to north. The letters appear in the configuration of the hills and valleys. They were there during Canaanite times, before Israel, as was Yehovah. Then His Presence moved from Mt. Sinai, to the Ark of the Covenant and next resided in Jerusalem in the Temple's Holy of Holies. I am explaining to you that the Almighty has written His Name on the mountains just below the place in *eretz Israel* known as Beit 'el, the House of God. If no one has proclaimed His Name, then the rocks will cry out His Name.

Chapter 6

Torah Has No Peer, Even Classical Greek Thinkers Astounded

Thirty five hundred years ago the Almighty directed Moshe to gather the nation of Israel near the base of Mount Sinai in the land of Midian. He cautioned on pain of death that each person or animal must avoid nearness to the mountain, on pain of death. Shofars were heard from the mountaintop but no one was up there and the entire mountaintop was on fire. After days of detailed preparations, the people were told to approach the mountain. The ground beneath their feet began shaking more and more violently. They all feared for their lives. The Almighty spoke and His voice was heard by each person as coming from out of the fire. Everyone heard the first Ten of His Words in the voice of Yehovah.[44] At the end of this first day *no one* ever wanted to go back to the base of the mountain. The people petitioned Moshe to request that the remainder of Yehovah's speech be given to Moshe alone. Hearing this request from Moshe, Yehovah agreed to this arrangement saying that the people had spoken well. The arrangement was that the people agreed to be obedient to whatever Moshe brought back down off Mount Sinai without knowing ahead of time what the scope of the instructions would be! (Would you buy a house with zero knowledge of *any* of its details?) This act constitutes the nation of Israel's agreement to allow Yehovah to rule over their individual lives and

---

[44] *Deuteronomy 4, 12. The Ten Commandments.*

for all time. They made Him their Ruler. He was already their Savior because He had delivered them from bondage at the hand of the Egyptian Pharaoh. We read elsewhere that Yehovah says, " there is no savior but Me".[45] These Ten Words that the people heard in Yehovah's voice are remembered as the Ten Commandments because they are the only teachings heard in Yehovah's voice personally by every individual Israelite. From counts of the thirteen tribes in "Numbers", Torah mentions the number of warriors which implies the nation to be approximately 2 million + people. What other pre television event in history has ever had 2 million personal eyewitnesses? So:

Torah, Dictated in the Voice of Yehovah

In contrast to Torah, the religions of the world collectively represent man's attempt to reach up to the Almighty in terms that humans find agreeable. Religions desire to please God but on human terms. This is upside down. Western religions have constructed their own scriptures descending from Yehovah's Words of Torah. Other self appointed humans then declare the new document to be holy. In contrast, Torah arrived in speeches in the voice and from the mind of Yehovah. The Ten Words were designed and elaborated throughout Torah in such a way as to bring about the end of evil deeds and injustice in the land of Israel and ultimately upon the entire earth. Over the next 40 years, Yehovah gave additional teachings, some face to face, to Moshe which are written in the five scrolls of Torah. These additional instructions filled out Yehovah's plan for implementation of the Ten Words. Leviticus is its heart. Torah's goal is not rigid compliance by everyone, but an end to evil, suffering and death on earth. **Rather than being The Law of the Land, it is the Solution of the Land.**[46] The struggle is not the moral question of good versus evil, but the supremacy of Torah in *eretz Israel*. This great cloud of witnesses to Torah's origin, plus the overriding instruction to not change Torah in any way including by any succeeding king of Israel, distinguishes Torah above that of all other "divine" documents *cultured* in western civilization.

Yehovah ordered that no one add or take away anything in Torah as given to Moshe. It is a complete teaching describing Yehovah's plan, it never has to be updated. It reflects Yehovah's holiness. He is holy, his Words are holy. It's for all time. What assurance is there that the Torah we have today has not been changed? One is found in its literary construction. In the ancient Hebrew Torah scrolls no small measure of resistance to change is provided by the following literary feat:

---

[45] *Isaiah 43, 11.*
[46] *Deuteronomy 11, 6 to 9. Read it now.*

Every 50th Hebrew letter in the first two sections (Genesis and Exodus) successively spell the word Torah. In the last two (Numbers and Deuteronomy) every 50th letter successively spells the word Torah backwards: "This way to the essence of Torah. You have passed the essence of Torah." Leviticus, the middle section or heart of Torah has a letter sequence in which every 7th letter spells the name of the Almighty. (I assure you it is not Lord. It is 𐤉𐤅𐤄𐤋, left to right, semitically. Right to left (western) it reads **yod hei vav hei**. Yehovah.) This literary **lock** against change is just one example of Torah's unique essence and here's why it is important:

The Leviticus scroll contains the worship instructions for the priestly tribe of Levi who are the descendants of the 13th tribe of Moshe and his older brother Aaron. (The 13th tribe has no land allotment.) A Levitical scribe making a new sheepskin copy of a Torah scroll is required to stop at the first letter of the name Yehovah and ceremonially wash, say prayers, ceremonially wash and write the first letter. Each letter of His Name requires this ceremonial rededication of the scribe. The Hebrew word for scribe is sofer, a word which means counter. So they counted words, right? No. Their counting system was more elaborate. They counted the letters and added them up as numbers. Each Hebrew character represents a letter and a number in their numbering system. (Also no two letters can even touch each other or they had to discard the entire copy and start over.) So the character numbers in a Torah copy have to numerically add up to those in the original! Other languages, including Greek, are really not designed for authenticating Torah copies, Hebrew is! Scribes are priests whose unique calling is to serve Yehovah through specific rituals intended to precisely reproduce the written Torah. Those are their priestly duties. In the letter inscriptions of Torah there are numerous creative embellishment such as Hebrew puns, variations in the font of the writing and aesthetic elaborations. Almost every opened section of scroll is embellished in some fashion. No embellishment can be omitted. Torah continues to be copied today in this exact tradition.

In the section in Exodus dealing with the escape from the Egyptians through the Yom Suf on dry land, the arrangement of letters on each side looks like a brick wall: each line starting and ending with the same letter so as to resemble the walls of water on each side of the dry land. *Any* change would be obvious. Meaning would be compromised. The point is that confidence is high that in 3500 years Torah copies remain faithful to what was written down by Moshe after he heard directly from Yehovah. Gentiles dismiss Torah as if it were a worn out old shoe.

In the Shrine of the Book museum in Jerusalem there is a sacred vault containing fragments of original Torah scrolls found at Qumran archeological site. This Torah is 1,000 years earlier than any previous Torah scrolls in existence. For some years Torah experts have been studying them using infra red technology to resolve any questions arising from water marks, tears etc. Their conclusion is that the Hebrew Torah scrolls in use today are exactly the same as the 2,000 year old Torah from Qumran. This dates this Torah to the time of Jesus. Jesus accepted Torah of his day as equal to the original written by Moses. **Yehovah**!

Human beings tend to value highly what they have just created as new and innovative. Few seek the ancient paths Torah describes as the Good Way. Few take the time to examine their personal beliefs and behavior in relation to a three thousand year old anything. For gentiles living in a pagan nation half way around the earth from Israel, there are several Torah truths that stand out as being particularly important to know and observe.

After Yehovah gave His Torah at Mount Sinai, He gave Moshe other torahs while the people followed Yehovah's cloud forty years in the desert. When the cloud moved, they moved. Yehovah spoke a torah about the 7th day of the week.

On the sixth day they gathered twice as much bread (manna), two 'omers' per person; and all the community leaders came and reported to Moshe. He told them, " This is what Adonai has said: 'Tomorrow is a holy Shabbat for Adonai. Bake what you want to bake; boil what you want to boil; and whatever is left over, set aside and keep for the morning.'" They set aside till morning, as Moshe had ordered; and it didn't rot or have worms. Moshe said, "Today, eat that; because today is a Shabbat for Adonai; Today you won't find it in the field. Gather it six days, but the seventh day is the Shabbat; on that day there won't be any." However, on the seventh day, some of the people went out to gather and found none.

Adonai said to Moshe, "How long will you refuse to observe my mitzvot and teaching? (Then Moshe said) Look, Adonai has given you the Shabbat. This is why he is providing bread for two days on the sixth day. Each of you, stay where you are; no one is to leave his place on the seventh day."[47]

The Sabbath torah is unique in that not only was it given to the nation of Israel before they received Torah, its principle predates man himself. It mirrors the Almighty's work in constructing the universe over a six *day* period followed by one period of rest. The Hebrew perspective is that observance of Sabbath is **the** indicator of one who observes Torah. This Shabbat torah was given to the Hebrews on the 6th day of the week (a day called Friday in the western world). The Sabbath started that eventide. A biblical day runs from just before one sundown to the next sundown.

For hundreds of years following the speaking of Torah from Mt. Sinai,

---

[47]*Exodus 16, 23 to 29.*

Hebrews categorized all the peoples of the earth as either **"righteous"** or **"sinners"**. The righteous had Yehovah's Torah and were observant of it in their everyday lives. Everyone else was called a sinner because they were ignorant of Torah and lived their lives without it. This is the true, biblical meaning of the word *sinner*. During this period of time, starting perhaps around 1450 years B.C.E., the Israelites worshiped Yehovah totally by Torah alone. All of the worship was practiced according to Yehovah's Torah instructions. There were no sects of the righteous. There was no Judaism. All were righteous by Torah. All issues of worship, as well as civil and criminal matters were resolved by Torah. There was no criminal justice system, no courts, no police and no jails: just the priest, the people and Torah. This singular Torah culture lasted hundreds of years. Sinners and words in later Scriptures such as evil, unfaithful, adulterous, pagan and foreigner all refer to those living life without Torah. All of these terms refer to any standards not conforming to Torah. These Torahless distinctions are still applicable today. Torah remains unchanged. Sinners are adulterous only in that they live in pagan ways as opposed to Torah ways. Torah says we shall have "no other gods before Me". This also means that when we appear before Yehovah at His appointed times we shall have within us no vestiges of pagan gods which we bring with us into the Presence of His face.

For perhaps 3,000 years Yehovah communes with His people on the seventh day of the week. Today, Torah observant people world wide still meet with Him on that day. Millions of Torahless people show up to worship Him the next day, a day called SUN day which honors Constantine's false sun god *sol invictus Mithra*. In so doing they place a pagan god in Yehovah's face and place one of His servants under worship.[48] When one identifies a broken *mitzvah* [49] in his life the thing to do is to double back to the words of Yehovah.[50] If you go through Christianity's beliefs one by one checking for **Torahless** paganisms and dropping them out of your life, you will have quite a job ahead of you. What bedrock is left behind? You will know the Almighty's Name: Yehovah; You will have His Torah from which you may know and understand Yehovah; You may seek to be a sojourner with Israel; You have chosen the ancient Ways of Yehovah over the sayings of men. Consider people who have examined Christianity and discarded it settling on doctrines of World Peace or revering the environment. A doctrine is the way in which one conducts their everyday, personal life. It is not just a "theory". For some such doctrines as world peace and environment serve as their religion. For me, neither world peace nor the

---

[48] *Deuteronomy 4, 15 to20.*
[49] *A command or good deed. A life principle of behavior.*
[50] *Jeremiah 6, 16; also 19b and 20.*

environment are large enough issues. Only Yehovah can establish and maintain world peace and that is His plan. Human hands are not needed. I do not care to cross Him by worshiping parts of creation. However I do understand the desire to find something better than organized religion.

In Torah we have the best copies man can devise and reproduce, not versions. Torah stands authenticated by the thriving nation of Israel in the modern world. For Christians, Jesus' use as the authority for his teachings, links them solidly with Torah. Sometimes in literature we have to settle for a copy because the original signed by the author is no longer with us. Abraham Lincoln's handwritten Gettysburg Address from which he read while actually giving the speech at Gettysburg is no longer available. By request after the speech, he made several handwritten verbatim copies available for sale in order to raise money for the government and other worthy causes. The copy displayed by the U.S. government is one of those later copies. Confidence is high that this authenticated copy was penned and signed by him and is in fact a true copy. It is not a revision, but is as authentic as the original. Thus it is with Torah we have today. In the case of the Torah, the original stone tablets made by God were destroyed and Moshe provided a second set that was written by God's finger. Moshe had to supply the second set of stone tablets, but it was still in God's handwriting: a signature original, as are Lincoln's Gettysburg Address copies.

In the case of the world's oldest and most copied book the Bible, it is a fact that the original writings of the ancient authors (their signature documents) are no longer available. Over the course of several thousand years the sheepskin media deteriorated. It is copies or nothing. For those who believe that their Christian Bible is the inspired Word of God, divine inspiration could only be true for the signature originals since the divine birth of a divine document can only be a one time event in the passage of time. None of the English bibles in the world have any possibility of being the original Word of God as they are not even in the same language. The Torah we have today remains in its Semitic languages of Hebrew and Aramaic. The characters, that is the individual written letters themselves have undergone numerous transformations in appearance over the last 3500 years. However, each letter has its same individual identity and significance.

The history of western religion is the story of how powerful men throughout the ages have used various techniques of creating grey areas, room for interpretation and linguistic cracks in the Almighty's Torah. That surely is true of Christianity. Nevertheless, the Almighty's Will moves dynamic human events to His fruition, no matter how harmful and damaging to individuals who are caught up in His activities.

Events in human history always move back to His plan. It is a relentless tide of power which forces the universe to conform to His plan no matter how far off His path the rulers of mankind have moved historical events. For example, it was the announced will of the Almighty that His people be free from slavery to the Egyptian Pharaoh. The reason given in Torah is that while slaves, they were not allowed to worship Him in the manner in which He desired. This scenario is still true today. A large part of humanity is not being allowed to worship Yehovah according to His Torah instructions. They are being held captive by foreign religious practices at odds with the way the Israelites worshiped Yehovah during the first millennia of Torah when there were no sects among the Hebrews.

The time is coming when the Almighty will do away with all religions and cause His Torah to rule the earth in total world wide peace. Do we need to say again **God Hates Religion**? We all know the outcome of the first captivity in Egypt: Yehovah 1, Pharaoh 0. Did you know that the remnants of Pharoah's army of chariots including a wheel from his own four spoked golden wheeled chariot has been found lying in the bottom of the Yam Suf?[51] It's been preserved there for 3500 years waiting to be revealed to us in modern times. I have underwater video (obtained from Messianic teacher Michael Rood) of Pharoah's army of chariots spread over about a mile and a half lying on the bottom of the crossing site.[52] So much for all the foreigner experts who say the crossing site is either lost or somewhere else. This and other archaeological evidence, when understood via a Hebraic perspective, put us on notice that Torah's account of the Almighty's activities here on earth is affirmed.

There is other credible evidence of the unique character of Torah not only as a religious foundational document but also as the unequaled foundation of ancient philosophy and civilization.

Greeks ranked Moses with Hermes and Plato!

As the assumptive author of Torah and as the leader of the nation of Israel during the exodus from Egypt, Moshe has been the most highly regarded of all Jews in history. Torah reports Moshe spoke face to face [53] with Yehovah yet he was the most humble man who ever lived. The impact of Moses on the rest of the ancient world, specifically the Greek philosophers should be realized even by those of us who turn down our noses at ancient Greek mythology and polytheism. Unlike the

---

[51] *Exodus 15, 4 and 5.*
[52] *Deuteronomy 7, 10 to 15.*
[53] *Numbers 12, 6 to 8.*

civil codes of all other civilizations, Torah reserved capital penalty (death) for crimes resulting in loss of human life. It excluded property crimes. (A corollary of Yehovah's description of the Sanctity of Life: Man is created in God's Image). The Greek's were seduced by what they believed to be Moshe's novel approaches to civilized national legislation.

The ancient Greeks ranked Moshe high among their own mythological gods, legendary figures and classical thinkers. They believed that his Torah writings and miracles demonstrated that he was descended from the divine and was thus equal to Hermes. While all other ancient civil and religious codes originated by the authority of a sovereign king or Pharaoh, Torah uniquely proceeded from the monotheistic authority of Moshe's God, the Creator of the Universe. Greek thinkers found divine inspiration of national legislation to be a most compelling new theory. How lamentable it is that they lifted up the name of Moshe but did not give any credence to Moshe's acknowledgment of the Creator of the Universe as the true intelligent Mind who *dictated* His Torah to Moshe. **Men still make the same mistake.**

The Greeks credited Moshe with inventing Hebrew writing. (Bit of a stretch, though possible). They revered him as the inventor also of Phoenician script, and in this way, of Greek writing (bigger stretches, reflecting cultural adaptations).

Many ancient Greek writers honored Moshe's considerable influence upon their thinking. Eupolemas, the earliest Hellenistic Jewish historian, writing with a very small Greek vocabulary and in poor syntax to Greeks, admired Moshe as the first wise man in all of mankind's ancient history. The Greeks dismissed the Hebraic context of Moshe's Torah writings in favor of viewing his persona only in the context of their own system of mythological gods and heroes. It is as if they didn't really believe in any true higher power, only in human creations of gods. In *God Hates Religion* a major theme is that the western religions descended from Torah have likewise dismissed Hebraic context of Torah as Yehovah's intentional context of His message. Here the Greeks manifested traditions of cross-cultural assimilation of a one of a kind sublime writing, completely disregarding the existence of the Author.

The writer Numenius of Apamea, (who wrote of three gods "Father", "Creator" and "Created" who were *one*!!!),[54] opined that Plato was merely a Greek speaking Moses! Both Homer and Hesiod were inspired by Moshe's writings. The first century Jewish historian Josephus claimed Moshe to be the first world class legislator. Philo accused other classical philosophers and legislators as too freely

---

[54] *Is the Christian concept of **Trinity** a Hellenic mythological construct?*

borrowing Moshe's (*Yehovah's really*) teachings on civil proceedings. The Hebraic view of Torah adopted here asserts that the teachings of Torah differ completely from Egyptian and ancient Greek "theories" of both religion and government. Understood within its Hebraic context, Torah stands alone. The foundations of ancient western civilization owe their wisdom not to revered ancient teachers such as Plato, but to the wisdom of Yehovah. Likely, Yehovah allowed the self importance of their own identities as legendary Greek thinkers to preclude them from acknowledging in humility that which Moshe's words, placing Torah directly in their faces, routinely identified Yehovah as the divine Person and Creator of the universe.

Torah has no peer as the world's premier national legislative document. However that was not its purpose. The nation of Israel is a nation of witnesses both of Torah's truly divine origin and of Yehovah's presence among them. Torah has no peer in the extreme care with which it has been copied and passed down to us. It has no peer in its many novel solutions to civilized legislation which is freely admitted by numerous of the classical Greek "thinkers". Like the ancient Greeks, the modern western religious world completely disregards the facts of Yehovah including His warnings to not change His Words.

Chapter 7
Semitic Sources of
NT scriptures

Here are a few of the many documents witnessing the original writing of the NT books in Aramaic or Hebrew and later translated into Greek. In Israel's National Library in Jerusalem there are most if not all of the Semitic sources of the NT microfilmed from world wide sources including the Dead Sea scrolls (2nd century B.C.E.). And for time line comparison, the Aleppo Codex (a 10th century C.E. copy of the Tanakh) resides in the Israel Museum in Jerusalem. It was rated by Nehemiah Gordon as the most important manuscript of the Tanakh.

The Cardinal of Rome issued a decree of Inquisition on September 9, 1553 (Rosh Hashana) banning the Talmud. Since the authorities could not read Hebrew, they confiscated everything written in Hebrew. Later, Jean duTillet, the Bishop of Brieu, France was visiting Rome and was very surprised to find a copy of Matthew written in the Hebrew language. For more than 1200 years NO ONE believed that any NT book had ever been written in any language other than Greek or Latin. On inspection duTillet was astounded to find that it predated any known copies of Greek or Latin "originals". He placed the Hebrew Matthew in the Biblioteque Nationale, Paris where it remains to this day. This library has historically contained the world's largest collection of Semitic texts of ancient Hebrew scriptures.

A Swiss Hebrew and Aramaic linguist and geography teacher named Sebastian Munster used dissections of his own ancient copy of Matthew as examples for his linguistic teachings. They were written in ancient Hebrew. By popular request, he reassembled the sections and published his copy in 1537. Posthumously a second edition was published in 1557. The 1557 edition also contained an appendix with an ancient Hebrew text of Hebrews.[55] It agrees 99% with the duTillet Hebrew Matthew.

Johannes Quin Quarboreus (A.K.A. Jean Cinquarbres), a linguist colleague of Munster, possessed multiple sources of Matthew in Hebrew. Cinquarbres possessed Munster's notes documenting in detail the restoration of his reassembled sections. The notes reveal that the "restoration" was merely cutting and pasting. Munster did not publish these notes with his printed Matthew leading many ignorant scholars to later incorrectly discount his ancient copy of Matthew. Cinquarbres published his own Hebrew version of Matthew in Paris in 1551. From his references to "the ancient author" it is clear that he believed his Matthew to be a faithful copy of the Semitic original.

Shem Tob Ben Yitz'chak Ben Shaprut was a Spanish Jew who lived during the Spanish Inquisition. To provide "talking points" for his fellow Jews during the Inquisition, he wrote *Even Bohan* meaning test stone. A test stone traditionally was used in certifying weights in commercial weights and measures: a Torah requirement. The inference is that Hebrew Torah is the standard or test stone by which all other Scripture must be measured. In those days of the notorious Spanish Inquisition, a local Catholic bishop would have the local rabbi taken to a public trial called a *disputation* where the rabbi would have to defend his trust in the Torah. If he loses he may be executed. If he prevails he is subject to deportation. Included in *Even Bohan* was the addition of a primitive Hebrew text (test stone) of Matthew. The original (signature) document of *Even Bohan* is lost. Several copies of the manuscript have survived from the 1400s through the 1600s and all include the primitive Hebrew Matthew appended to them. Shem Tov's Matthew has been extensively studied by linguists George Howard and Nehemiah Gordon.[56] It contains far too many Hebrew elements to have been translated into Hebrew from any Greek original. How could numerous Hebrew jokes, puns on Hebrew words sounds or meanings, possibly get into an earlier Greek "original" version of the writing? The Greek language obviously does not contain idiomatic sayings which are Hebrew jokes. Greek puns are plays on the sounds and meanings of Greek words. Both expert linguists agree that a large amount of Shem Tob's Matthew had been "corrected" by someone who knew only a Latin version during the middle ages, possibly a ninth century monk. These "corrected" parts differ from the duTillet and

---

[55] *The reader is directed to many web sites on the internet where one can view copies of these documents. Some are freely downloadable and others may be purchased. Start with the word duTillet or go to TorahResources.com.*
[56] **The Hebrew Yeshua vs. the Greek Jesus** *by Nehemiah Gordon, ch. 7.*

Munster manuscripts. The rest of it, the uncorrected part is the original Hebrew.

One ancient Aramaic NT manuscript was discovered in a monastery in Naton Lakes Valley, Egypt by Dr. William Cureton in 1842. It is dated to between the 100s and the 300s C.E.. It includes all four Gospels. A second manuscript was found by Mrs. Agnes Smith Lewis at the St. Catherine's Monastery at the base of the traditional Mount Sinai in Egypt.[57] Both the Cureton and Lewis manuscripts are known as the Old Syriac Gospels. Both are written in ancient Aramaic. In 1858 Dr. Cureton published his manuscript saying that one Gospel is a copy of the actual ancient Aramaic text which is the work of the Apostle Matthew. I have two of Smith Lewis' books. They are difficult but rewarding to read. She was fluent in Aramaic. It is evident that she was a captive of her Christian religious beliefs as after all her work uncovering these ancient Aramaic Gospels, she failed to grasp that they predated all Latin and Greek copies.

The NT of the Peshitta (that is the original Syriac or Aramaic) was added to the Peshitta Tanakh before the writing of 2 Peter, 2 John, 3 John, Jude and Revelation. That dates the Peshitta's NT early in the first century. We could speculate they were closer to the original source writings and therefore not subjected to the same degree of errors via extraneous input. The Peshitta Tanakh may date as early as the time of Solomon (966 B.C.E.). It is in Aramaic. The Peshitta NT was copied by the Eastern Christian Church, in Aramaic and according to the same rules of accuracy as the Torah. That is not true of any other versions of the NT. All Peshitta texts world wide agree 100% with each other. The word *peshitta* means correct, straight or authentic.

A manuscript purchased by the Earl of Crawford in 1860 is a complete Peshitta text which includes the missing epistles and Revelation mentioned above. Many linguists have concluded that the underlying text is the original Aramaic.

There are many other sources which witness the Semitic language origins of

---

[57] *The Torah reports that Mt. Sinai where Moshe received the Torah is located in the land of Midian, which is present day Saudi Arabia. Fascinating video footage, more than a dozen hours, has been entrusted to Messianic teacher Michael Rood who has made it available for purchase. It supports the Saudi Arabia location with great detail. He has underwater footage of Pharaoh's army of chariots at the crossing site of the Yom Suf with King Schlomo's memorial poles marking the site. He has film of Sodom and Gomorrah's sites. I have a piece of brimstone from the site. All these concrete examples have been left for us to see so that we would not have to take these actions by the Almighty on faith by hearsay from someone else who also was not there.*

all the NT books. The church fathers of both the western and eastern churches all agreed that Matthew was written by him in his native Aramaic tongue. Clement of Alexandria said that Paul wrote Hebrews in Hebrew and later it was "carefully" ? translated by Luke into Greek for use by Greek speaking believers in Greece. See, you can dismiss all this Semitic information, but "creative" efforts are required pass off the original Semitic writings as originally written in the Greek language.

Talmudic rabbis have implied that the writings called "the gospels" were first in Hebrew or Aramaic. While they wanted to destroy these NT writings, but they could not because the writings contained the explicit Name of HaShem, יהוה. The Jewish historian Flavius Josephus who lived from 37 to 100 C.E. wrote that Aramaic was the language of first century Jews to the extent that none could speak nor read Greek. However Hellenized Hebrews existed earlier than 275 B.C.E. since the first Greek translation of Torah (Septuagint) was achieved by Hebrew elders in only 72 days in Alexandria, Egypt. Thousands of ossuaries (bone boxes) found in first century burial sites in caverns underneath Jerusalem have the mark of Yeshuaites and all have inscriptions written in Aramaic. **No one** buries their family loved one and then marks it with an epitaph scribed in a reviled foreign language.

Finally, in 1498 a Portuguese Roman Catholic "army" was deployed into India where it encountered 100 churches along the coast of Malabar using the actual Semitic NT which had been brought to them by the Apostle Thomas 1400 years earlier from Jerusalem!

There is a large body of witness to the Semitic origins of the NT writings. If you wish to see this with your own eyes, look at *www.torahresource.com/Dutillet*. Unlike the versions sourced from the Greek, these Hebrew writings are faithful to Torah's terminology. Unlike Torah they do not have an elegant appearance of fine literary penmanship. It is quite evident from their appearance that they have been reproduced in a crude fashion. They are only informal letters. They are plain in comparison with the beauty of all of Torah's features. Yet there is an unending amount of argument from believers, many of them scholars, who dogmatically cling to the theory of Greek origins of the NT. In the grand scale of Yehovah's universe, Greek translation equals Torahlessness, NO Torah. In the Hebrew Matthew, one of the last few messages Yeshua is reported to have uttered is: *"Depart from me all you workers of Torahlessness."*

Chapter 8

Sayings of Adonai Dishonored

The Almighty tells His chosen people to go to a distant land and upon arrival kill all the current inhabitants of it including men, women and children.[58] **THESE** are the words of Adonai? Why would the Almighty say such a thing? Long before the events just footnoted and previously described to you from Ezekial, He ordered the Hebrews to remove all evidence of foreign religions from His land. Does that sound like the God is Love persona that has been for years taught by the Christian church? Apparently, He really really does not want foreign religions on His land. The Almighty continued with His instructions to Israel as to how they are to take over the land He promised Abraham. He says that He will place fear in the current inhabitants and so guarantee the Israelite victory over inhabitants whose cultures will not survive into modern times. (Evidently one of His methods, was to allow the nation of Israel under different leaders to cross both a sea and a river on dry land. This alarming information about the power of the Israelite God spread legendarily throughout the gentile nations resulting in FEAR of Israel.) Yehovah ordered Israel to doom certain pagan inhabitants to destruction and totally demolish all remnants of their foreign worship practices. His people were not to intermarry so that none of these foreign paganisms could continue in the land of Israel. (Deuteronomy 7, 1 to 11). Before we criticize King Solomon for marrying a daughter of Pharoah, we should find out if our particular church organization has any outposts in Jerusalem or elsewhere in Eretz Israel. To continue, at the very least and

---

[58]*Deuteronomy 2, 30 to 35; 3,2 and 3; and Joshua 6, 21.*

relative to the Promised Land: God hates religion. He wants it all totally wiped out from His land and among His people for the same reason that He delivered (*saved*, as in Isaiah 43, 11) His people from bondage in Egypt: So that they would be free to worship Him on His land and according to His instructions given to Moses. Simple, clear, unchanged will.

This book throughout elaborates how millions of faithful Christian believers down through the centuries have not worshiped Him according to the instructions in Moshe's Torah. Rather, religious traditions of men contradict the expressed sayings of Yehovah.[59] We live in a time when the gentiles ruling a major branch out of Judaism is decreasing. Christianity's numbers are shrinking. The largest revival in human history is prophesied to occur in this millennia. Post biblical (NT) prophetic scripture says this revival will be accomplished by twelve thousand members from each of twelve tribes of Yisrael. The only role of gentile believers therefore, would seem be that of those to be revived. The 144,000 Israelites will be teaching the Torah of the Almighty from the unique Semitic knowledge and perspective which they enjoy as a blessing of the Almighty. In Deuteronomy 33,4 it says Moses commanded a law for us (Torah) and it is the heritage of the congregation of Jacob, meaning the nation of Israel. The man Jacob renamed Israel is the man whose descendants are the congregation. Deuteronomy 32, 21 says a no name people, a "nation" of fools will vex Israel to jealousy. Could this prophetically be western Christian culture? Western gentile Christians have discarded His Name for foreign words. All of Christianity for 1900 years has evolved from Greek translations which substituted pagan polytheistic language and culture for the Almighty's choice of Hebrew and Aramaic. In Torah, Yehovah calls this type of substitution an abomination (Deuteronomy 12, 29 to 31). Abomination is the ultimate disgust, it surely is not tolerance. Deuteronomy 7, 25 and 26 speak of the abomination of foreign gods. It tells us we are to utterly detest and abhor their worship practices as an accursed thing. Anyone who brings an abomination into His house is doomed to the same destruction as the abominated thing. Thus avoiding abominations is a life and death issue. Yeshua observed:

> **"The reason you go astray is you are ignorant ....of the Tanakh...."** [60]

The Tanakh was Yeshua's bible. An example, the Christian church interprets the song of the Lamb in Revelation as scriptural evidence that Yeshua will some day be raised up and worshiped (Revelation 15, 3 and 4). However this song links to

---

[59] *Isaiah 29, 13.*
[60] *Matthew 22,29. Complete Jewish Bible. Tanakh is OT or large Torah.*

another, the Song of Moshe from Deuteronomy 32. There it appears Moshe is raised up and worshiped. However, the Torah facts are that Moshe sang the song to the people in worship of Yehovah. It was not Moshe singing a song to revere himself. Similarly the Song of the Lamb will be sung by the Lamb to Yehovah. It will not be sung to the Lamb in worship of the Lamb. Both songs are sung in praise of Yehovah. A Hebraic perspective reveals this true circumstance, church teachings do not. Hence we should worship Yehovah, not Yeshua. Revelation, and indeed the entire NT only have meaning as fulfillment of Torah. If you do not understand the purpose of the Song of Moshe, you will err in your interpretation of the song of the Lamb. You also misinterpret the function of the Lamb. Perhaps Yehovah will give you some slack. After all, you have been lied to[61] by experts and by a hundred generations of believers caught up in the paganization of Scriptures into foreign bibles. Later this book details the incorporation of foreign worship practices into the "sacred" traditional practices of Christianity. By the way, the entire Song of Moshe is quoted in the morning service at the synagogue. It is referred to extensively during the daily recitations of the Sh'ma. Sh'ma ("God is One") was practiced by Yeshua three times daily throughout his life. Jesus was a monotheist; There is no possibility that he believed in the trinity. The church does not teach Yeshua's recitation of the Sh'ma. Have you ever attended a Christian church that recites the Sh'ma? I haven't. See, gentile churches have no idea at all what they are talking about.

We have all heard people respond to information regarding the biblical (Torah) shortcomings of Christian teachings with: "I don't care what you say. I have Jesus in my heart and I know that I have a personal relationship with Him. He is my best Friend. Nobody has all the answers. I am under Grace, not the law and nothing you can say will change that so I am not going to change to your ideas." [62] These are direct recitations of church teachings, polemic reproductions. There are several difficulties with that thinking. First, none of these are my ideas. I think it is wonderful that you have a close personal experience with the Almighty. You should know what created the basis for your personal relationship with Yehovah including your avenue of prayer. At Mt. Sinai about 3500 years ago, two million people comprising the nation of Israel heard the Voice of the Almighty speak to each of them out of the fire, the cloud and the darkness. Each Israelite person heard the voice of God speak Ten Words (Commandments). THAT is Yehovah making religion personal. Next, there is no way for me to know the truth about God because of what

---

[61] *Jeremiah 16, 19b. The gentiles shall come to You from the ends of the earth and say " Surely our fathers have inherited lies, Worthless and unprofitable..."*
[62] *See Law in the Glossary chapter.*

you are feeling. There is no way for you to witness the teachings of God based only on your feelings. To follow your witness, I would have to worship you. I do not feel like worshiping you, I worship Adonai Eloheinu Yehovah. Also, don't Christians have in the NT an oft quoted verse which says that no scripture is of private interpretation? Lastly, if you consider Jeremiah 6, 16 and 17 you will read where the Almighty provided the path of Torah and asked the people to follow it for their own good. The response both times was "we will not". Here you are telling me that you will not choose the path of Torah. This book spends a fair amount of time linking Yeshua and Torah. Our church teachings have painted us into a corner. We need the Semitic perspective to float our way out back to following Yeshua's Torah lifestyle.

One of the last things Yeshua himself is recorded to have said at the end of his life on earth is about the coming Great Day. He is speaking as the son of man (a prophet) and as the fulfillment of Torah in human flesh; As the mouthpiece of Yehovah. We know that because the prophets have a past history of functioning as the mouthpiece of Yehovah beginning way back in Deuteronomy and running all through the Tanakh. In Matthew 7, 21 to 23 Yeshua says this:

"It is not everyone who merely says to me, My Lord, my Lord, who will enter into the kingdom of heaven, but he who does the will of my Father [63] in heaven. A great many will say to me in that day, My Lord, my Lord, did we not prophesy in your name and in your name cast out devils and in your name do many wonders: Then I will declare to them, I have never known you; keep away from me, O you that work iniquity." [64]

The words work iniquity are code for not following Torah. These words of Yeshua say that people call on *Yeshua's* name in vain (Psalm 91, 14 says this: Know My Name **Yehovah** or else). Here Yeshua points instead to doing the will of the Father which is obedience to Torah, Deuteronomy 10, 12 and 13. The main issue here is not whether we know the Almighty: it is DOES HE KNOW US? Do the Father's will (observe His Torah) and He does know you. When everyone finally has Torah in their heart there will be no need for anyone to teach others about Yehovah. Everyone will know Him. At that time will there be a function for religion? Yehovah will rule the world by Torah. For now, warnings about replacing Torah occur throughout the Scriptures. Christians routinely assume that because they feel right down to the core of their being that they know the Almighty, then it must also

---

[63] *This expression refers to he who observes for example Yahweh's Feasts.*
[64] *Matthew 7, 21 to 23. Holy Bible From the Ancient Eastern Text translated from the Aramaic Peshitta by George Lamsa.. Note that he chose, in the 1930s to express the name of God as Lord.*

be true the He knows them. Who knows why they ignore this obvious warning from the one even they call Almighty God? The Christian church's habit of picking and choosing teachings causes their followers to **over assume** their status in the grand scheme of Yehovah's Plan. Yehovah's method of operation is not hidden on this issue.

Time after time He tells His people not to enquire of the other inhabitants of the Promised Land as to how they worship their gods and then apply those worship practices to Him with the idea that they are doing it out of respect for Him. All those remnant whispers of foreign worship were supposed to have been wiped off the land. Here are some samples of these "do not enquire" torahs in the New King James Version. Because of the sojourner factor these apply to observant gentiles:

" **1. These are the statues and judgments which you shall be careful to observe in the land which the Lord God of your fathers is giving you to possess, all the days that you live upon the earth. 2. You shall utterly destroy all the places where the nations which you shall dispossess served their gods, on the high mountains and on the hills and under every green tree. 3. And you shall destroy their altars, break their sacred pillars, and burn their wooden images with fires; you shall cut down the carved images of their gods and you shall destroy their names from that place. 4. You shall not worship the Lord you God with such things."** [65]

"**..take heed to yourself that you are not ensnared to follow [the dispossessed nations presently living in the Promised Land], after that they are destroyed from before you, and that you do not enquire after their gods, saying, ' How did these nations serve their gods: I also will do likewise.' You shall not worship the Lord your God that way; for every abomination to the Lord [Me, Yehovah] which He hates they have done to their gods; for they burn even their sons and daughters in the fire to their gods."** [66]

"**And Elohim spoke all these Words, saying: I am [Yehovah] your [Elohim], who brought you out of the land of Egypt , out of the house of bondage, You shall have no other gods before [in front of] Me."** [67]

"**And in all things that I have said unto you take you heed; and make no mention of the name of other gods, neither let it be heard out of your mouth."** [68]

Yehovah calls substituting pagan practices for His instructions an

---

[65] *Deuteronomy 12, 1 to 4. See also Exodus 23, 13; Deuteronomy 11, 26 to 28.*
[66] *Deuteronomy 12,30 and 31.*
[67] *Exodus 20, 1 to 3.*
[68] *Exodus 23, 13. No western gentile can keep this statute since western calendars name the days and months after foreign gods: Thursday = Thor's day.*

abomination. In other words He[69] loathes it as in God Hates Religion. Greek translations of the NT bring with it pagan worship concepts and practices. For example Yehovah's idea is that the Hebrews will have a Messiah, but the Greek translation points to not one but many christs. Messiah and christ are not interchangeable. The concept, even the very word christ is riddled with paganisms.

Torah speaks of foreigners who love Yehovah, His Torah and His people. He calls them "My Gentiles". A Torah keeping gentile is called in the Torah a *sojourner.* Torah provides that Yehovah's sojourners have all the Torah rights of a native person born in the land, so that there is only one Torah that applies to all His people. Can one be a Torah keeping Christian? Yes, easily: by reproducing Jesus' Torah lifestyle. The ancient Hebrew perspective identified anyone who is not of Jewish descent as a pagan. The term pagan refers to foreigners on the basis of the fact that they live their lives without Torah. That is the essential definition of *pagan*: no Torah. That is its only Scriptural connotation. (I have found it is not good to go around calling individual Christians pagans to their face, they interpret pagan differently.) If you escape from religion you will find that at first you will be down to only basic, grand scale realities: One, you know the Almighty's Name. The Name He calls Himself, spelled **yod hei vav hei**. Two, you have Torah. Three, if you are a gentile, you have a role to fulfill with your life: that of one of Yehovah's sojourners. No one can take those realities away. So, do not allow any pagan to judge you. Yehovah knows you.

Yeshua reportedly said that pure religion is assisting widows and orphans. If so, religion should be about giving. Too often it is in practice about controlling. In contrast Torah is in plain language, unequivocal in its concrete terms and its immunity to change. The true scriptural meaning of the term *sinner* is described by a concrete fact: NO TORAH. This is the basis for the related Torah term iniquity. It has nothing to do with all the complex schemes developed by later religions revolving around their descriptions of their mythological term sin. So, in the first millennia after receiving Torah, the Hebrews had no religion, only Torah. There were only two kinds of people worldwide: Hebrews who lived by Torah and foreigners who lived by what was right in their own eyes and worshiped god's of their own creations. Essentially that continues to be true today.

The Almighty has a plan to offer Torah to all the people of earth. When one reads Yehovah's plan in His words, the Christians among us will be surprised to find

---

[69] *All nouns in Hebrew are gendered either male or female.* **Yahweh** *is male, while Spirit of God,* **Ruach ha Kodesh***, is female.*

out that the role of gentile believers is vastly different from what has been taught to them by their church. Nowhere in Torah or Tanakh does Yehovah say that He has changed His mind about the identity of the beneficiaries of his covenant with Abraham: Israelites. In the Greek versions of the NT it appears He has changed His mind because new words in a different language have replaced the Aramaic words spoken in the actual events featured in the NT writings. Virtually all Christians have learned foreign interpretations of Yehovah's words. These interpretations are liberally seasoned with new foreign concepts not original to Torah, the standard for the NT. [70] One choice would be to let the Hebrews interpret the parts of the bible they have written and the gentiles interpret the parts they have written. Hint: there is a small number of writings in the Tanakh, less than TWO chapters written by a gentile. King Nebuchadnezzar apocalyptically gives his testimony in chapter 4 of Daniel. In it he reports experiencing a mental breakdown, eats grass, etc. It ends with him bowing to the Holy One of Israel and reiterating that the Most High humbles the most arrogant. The point is that a large part of this book involves detailed pagan church customs which an arrogant church will *some day* realize it will need to leave behind.

What you do with all this information is up to you. It does not change the author's relationship with Yehovah at all. The point is that the Greek descended versions of the NT are written in such a way as to obscure the fact of Yeshua's obedience to and teaching of Torah. If we look at how much of Acts covers the activities of Yeshua's brother, James the Just or. James the Righteous ("righteous" means "Torah keeper"), we come up with zero. Acts reports very little. Yeshua entrusted his brother James with his faithful flock of followers. James carried on the Torah centered teaching of Yeshua for the rest of his years and built Yeshuaite Torah observance into a multi national movement. He died in 62 C.E. None of his work is described in Acts and even his death is omitted in Acts. Acts is full of unidentified groups of Hebrews, all impugned by the derogatory label "Jews". Which Jews? The Rabbanites? The Priests of the Temple? The Pharisees? The Sadducees? The Yeshuaite believers in Yeshua from James and Peter's Jerusalem synagogue house of "upper room" fame? The Apostles? All these groups and the entire indigenous population of Israel were Jews. In concert with this, Paul's epistle writings redirect teaching away from Torah observance and towards a Torah breaking new gentile religious movement centered around a concept called *Gospel*. Gospel is Torah

---

[70] *[Consider the Bereans who were more noble than those in Thessalonika because the Bereans compared all new teachings to Torah on a daily basis to find out if what they have just heard is true]: Acts 17,10 and 11.*

altered. **The gospel cannot be the foundation of Torah (anachronism).**

One group taking exception to Paul's new teachings was those pesky Bereans who just would not give up clinging to Torah as their standard of truth. The fact is that for the first 30+ years after the passing of Yeshua, all leaders in the Jesus movement, including Peter and Paul reported to James. Either a huge chunk of original Acts writings was deliberately omitted in later years, perhaps during the switch from Aramaic to Greek, or Acts was totally rewritten to minimize James' continuation of Yeshua's Torah keeping teachings while favoring Paul's new gentile oriented Gospel. See more detail in the Co Stars chapter, but the point now is that James and the Bereans met the same NT scriptural fate. They were both deleted from scriptural history and it all falls at the feet of those who needed to exclude Yeshua's teaching of Torah observance in order to recruit gentiles into the Gospel religion.

Are New Teachings (Gospel) for gentiles a forbidden change to Torah? Gentile Christian believers claim to be grafted in to the family of God by Jesus. And the Messianics claim this via Yeshua, whom they believe to be the Messiah. But, Torah teaches that gentiles are grafted in by sojourning with Israel via Torah observance. And, Yeshua taught this same Torah observance. Yet the average Christian has always been told by his church "everything revolves around us. The Jews are out. We are in." This argument is known as Replacement Theology and an excellent teaching is available from the ministry of Jonathan Bernis, a long time Messianic teacher of Torah observance. Yehovah's apparent purpose for grafting in the gentile believers is revealed way back in Deuteronomy 32, 21 where a no name people are prophesied to VEX Israel prompting them to jealousy. Who could this " no name " people be? If the term refers to a band of people who do not have a name because they are not identified by their land nor are they one of the nations of the world, it could refer to the Christian church. Also the word Christian is not a word that is found in Torah. It is a foreign word. Gentiles living in Antioch, Syria developed the term to refer to the apostles. Thus Deuteronomy 32, 21 is also a prophecy. Parts of Deuteronomy are often quoted in Revelation. When Revelation is taught by churches via Hebraic Deuteronomy, it would lead us back to Yeshua's Torah teachings and back to Torah thus realigning the NT with Torah.

Torah v. Varieties of Bibles

What test standards could we use to rationally support our choice of which to believe: Semitic texts or Greek texts; Israel or The Church; Yehovah or Religions; Torah or Bibles; Yeshua and James or Paul. If we are testing anything to see what is best among baby strollers, tanks, cars, ships, aircraft, schools or religions we may choose on the basis of these criteria: 1) longevity; 2) reliability; 3) validity; 4) record of achievements; 5) functionality; 6) simplicity; 7) durability. Let us see how these seven criteria provide some measure of support for the claim that only Torah is the Word of God. If this looks like overkill to you, perhaps you can consider this a mid book summary:

1) Longevity. Has it withstood the test of time? Of all the "ites" who have dwelt on earth down through history, the only nation of "ites" still with us are the Israelites: the same peoples who revere Torah. Gone are the Amalakites, the Ammonites, Edomites, Jebusites, Hittites and all the other ites. Even the Egyptians are gone. Considering 3,000 years of anti Semitism and that they have always had the smallest population numbers of any of the "ites" their continued existence is truly remarkable. Today they are still surrounded by hostile nations, all of them much larger and more powerful. These facts validate Torah's account of Yehovah's historical intervention on behalf of the Hebrews. Lastly, Torah in use today in Israel is precisely the same as that used by Yeshua as his bible (evidence below). Is two thousand years of longevity long enough to be credible?

2) Reliability. Dependable consistency, steadfastly trusted. Is it always true to the description of its roots? Do you get the same story every time? There are some 34,800 denominations of Christianity and multiple versions and interpretations of each one's scriptures. There are arguably a half dozen sects of Judaism and several sects of Messianic believers but only one Torah for them all. Where is the reliable story when there are 33, 856 versions of biblical teachings? This speaks to the existence of millions of unreliable witnesses. The Torah proper, the first five books, has come down to us on Hebrew scrolls quite unchanged in their 3500 year existence. We have the Karaites, descendants of the first righteous Torah keepers to thank for that. There are safeguards in the construction of Torah's structure of Hebrew letters as well as procedures for the reproduction of its scrolls by scribes and these safeguards have made it possible for the Karaites to provide us with present day Torah true to the ancient writing of Torah. The other scrolls of the Writings and the Prophets share some safeguards of Torah but not those of its exquisite construction. **You have seen and will see for yourself later in the book how the NT absolutely fails in comparison to Torah's fidelity safeguards.**

3) Validity. Is it the genuine article, a legitimate original, signed by the originator or a true copy with absolute fidelity to the original? There are no surviving originals of any scroll in the Scriptures. Written on very thin animal skin parchment rolled up into scrolls, the average life span for these may have been 200 to 500 years. The earliest surviving written Torah scripture dated sometime before 601

B.C.E., is 600 years older than the dead sea scrolls. The Aaronic prayer (Numbers 6, 24 to 26) was found inscribed on two tightly rolled up silver amulets. (They were almost mistaken for cigarette butts.) This prayer passage in today's Torah is exactly the same. NASA analysis of the amulets in the 1990s identified the prayer scribed over the top of an even earlier saying from Deuteronomy 7!

Because of the existence of a code arrangement in the written Hebrew characters in the Torah, confidence is high that the author must have been the Almighty. The alternative is that we have all seriously underestimated the intelligence of the Jewish people. But even that conclusion leads us back to Yehovah. Where did they get all that intelligence? In contrast to the dozen or less Judaic and Messianic movements which cling to one written Torah from 3500 years ago, there are some 34,800 denominations of Christianity spinning off a multiple re translations of events chronicled to have occurred only 1,500 years ago. This shortsighted view arrogantly minimizes the only written history of any nation of peoples who can trace their ancestors by name all the way back to Adam. In the USA most cannot trace more than 400 years in ancestry.

4) Record of Achievements. Do subsequent events bear out the prophetic claims? Hebrew Scriptures are full of prophecies which have come true in human history. It is full of prophecies which have not yet come true. Presently it could be about half and half. Most of all, throughout the bible we see that anyone who has gotten on the wrong side of the Almighty has had himself and his ideas stamped out. In other words, the stampees have no surviving descendants, little ongoing achievements and no surviving culture. The mighty ancient Egyptians are gone. Modern peoples living in the land of Egypt are Arabs who are not related to the ancient Egyptians. But, the Hebrews have survived. And they have a striking record of world renowned achievements. Ninety per cent of the winners of the Nobel Peace Prize have historically been Jews.

5) Functionality. Do the Torah's rules for living result in a positive outcome? From God's standpoint they do, because as the Manufacturer He is providing human beings with the official owner's manual. Secondly Yehovah's Torah instructions are designed by Yehovah to end evil in the world and so create world peace. From the standpoint of human beings, the history of world wide anti Hebrew activity plays like a broken record. It is the revolving story of leaders of foreign nations who have seized the world's stage with some new kind of power that will enable them to once and for all totally exterminate the Jewish race from the face of the earth. ALL such attempts over the last 4,000 years have failed and their plans backfired on the perpetrators. Recently, Iran has set itself up for this exact scenario.

The Hebrew culture's adherence to Torah, apparently, has resulted in a race of people who over hundreds of generations have maintained superior intellectual capabilities. Up until a generation ago, it was true that 90 % of the winners of the Nobel Peace Prize have been Jewish individuals. There are more science and technology innovations from Jewish people than all other races combined. In the last generation or so, an anti Semitic world has awakened to this fact. Nowadays we are seeing Peace Prizes awarded to gentiles of fame according to vastly different criteria than what has been historically practiced. Yet, the current cutting edge of scientific and technological advances is not at Caltech, Berkeley nor M.I.T.: it's in Israel. Think about this. In developing their nuclear weapons technology, did Israel have to come to the USA with hat in hand? No, they did not. Let me given you a name: Samuel T. Cohen, the inventor of the short range tactical nuclear warhead. Short range meaning that the artilleryman can launch a nuclear payload with a small enough burst diameter so he lives to tell about it. Samuel T. Cohen is even more well known as the inventor of the neutron bomb. For some time he has been in charge of Israel's nuclear weapons research. The bottom line is that they do not really need our help. They probably have the ability to annihilate the entire middle east with no help from the USA; The ability but not the desire. Prophecy in Zechariah 5,1 says that nuclear war will come to the Middle East.

6) Simplicity. Is it in plain language? Can any person regardless of mental acuity or level of education readily understand the manner in which one is to conduct their life? The Torah demands that it's words be read aloud to the people every seven years. This is taken to mean that its words are understandable by seven year old children. It is so concretely worded that even the lowliest shepherd understands its meanings without needing to have it explained to him. This is genuine irony in comparison to the complicated wording of the many obtuse terms in the English biblical. If English translations were simple enough for a seven year old to understand, no one would have to go to a religion for help in knowing the meaning of its words. Hence, the English speaking religious world relies upon theological concepts: abstractions eluded by actual historical and physical reality. Years of intellectually inbred teaching of theological abstractions in Christianity are freely used to validate clergy teachings.

7) Durability. Resistance to degradation or change over time. Is today's Torah the same as the message the Almighty originally spoke to Moshe? There is the partial direct evidence (scientific analysis of the Dead Sea scrolls) that the Hebrew scrolls of the Torah are genuine, authentic and faithful to that in use during the life of Jesus. Yeshua accepted the Torah of his times as the authentic Torah of Moses.

Therefore today's Torah is authentic to both Jesus's and Moses'. The challenge for all of us is to find the best English translation of Torah available and so begin to understand the nuances of 3500 year old Torah statements given in a culture and language, parts of which are not very well understood these days.

Chapter 9

The Christian *NT*

It has troubled me for some time that Jesus never stopped what he was doing and found a scribe to write down his life story in his own Galilean Aramaic words. Such a deed would have defined his lifestyle and teachings for all time as unequivocally pro Torah. Apparently he was not interested in adding to Torah. Instead the task of telling his story fell to the memories of twelve fishermen who wrote letters to other people recollecting the events of Yeshua's life, prophecies and teachings. Letters? Contrast that with the exquisite construction of the Torah delivered to us with its internal safeguards against any changes. Did Yeshua intend for his followers to use his life and teachings as the basis for a new bible which would replace his bible, the Tanakh? Obviously not. Quotes of Scripture show that he considered the Tanakh in existence from 1500 years earlier to be the original Words of Yehovah. Letters from less educated fishermen would not seem to be a good method of ensuring that future generations would receive the upgrade for Torah known today as the Christian NT. Compared to Torah, the NT's construction lacks internal safeguards needed to protect it from change. It also contains none of the elegant literary embellishments so cleverly contained in Torah's writings. So either Yeshua was not the Torah changer the Christian church thinks him to be or he is being Torah observant. The present book, GHR, claims Jesus was completely Torah observant. Throughout the entire Christian NT it is reported that various people, notably Yeshua, recited quotes of Scripture which are all quotations from the Tanakh. If Yeshua meant for his believers to have a New Torah, why did he persist 100% of the time in going back to *old* passages in the ancient Tanakh as the authority for his assertions? Not the move of someone replacing Torah, is it? A very few words of his actual quotes of Tanakh persisted through subsequent translations in his original

Aramaic. These Aramaic quotes remained down through later translations in other languages down through history so that some Aramaic words are present even into today's English versions of NT.[71] This demonstrates his words spoken and written down in his native language of Aramaic, not Greek. Yeshua spoke in the Galilean dialect of the common language of almost the entire Middle East. In the time of Yeshua almost no Hebrew in the land of Israel spoke Greek with the known exception of Luke.[72] The fact is that no one, and I mean NO ONE can write in a language that he cannot speak. The NT events of the day were spoken in Aramaic and later written in both Aramaic and Hebrew.

So, if Yeshua meant for the new second half of the Christian bible, to replace the ancient Scriptures he routinely quoted, why didn't he write down the new ideas himself. His teachings often berated the changes to Torah made by rabbinic written oral traditions. Knowing his Father criminalized changes to Torah, Yeshua declared the ancient Rabbi's had made the Torah of no effect. Considering this, if he meant to create a new religion, he would have anticipated that future generations would also develop replacement traditions to change his own teachings.[73] Instead of a NT which replaces the "Old Testament" and is superior in every way to the Tanakh, we have a NT which is in most respects inferior. The 34,800+ sects of Christianity established themselves on the coat tails of foreign language interpretations of NT. Yeshua's unity prayer is certainly no foundation for 34,800 sects of ✝. Did Yeshua, Yehovah's anointed one, overlook an essential part of his ministry while here on earth? If he meant his teachings to become the replacement of Torah, Yeshua should have alerted his followers repeatedly of their sacred duty to write new scriptures that would replace Torah. He was silent on this whole subject. Why? Because he did nothing in violation of Torah. He spoke against replacing Torah.[74] **It is time for individual Christians to get a grip on the real Torah fulfilling Yeshua.**

There are other dilemmas: 1) While NT "books" were written by several authors, the most prolific (Shaul or Paul) was not even a follower of Yeshua! Holy land history shows he was a persecutor of Yeshua and was a Roman government informant, the opposite of a follower; 2) As Greek translations occurred, all the proper names of the people in the recorded NT events were changed; 3) References to Torah events in terms of the Jewish (connoting denigration) calendar were deleted.

---

[71]*"Eli, Eli, lama sabbachthani?" From Matthew 27, 46.*
[72]*See text near top of page 77.*
[73] *Hegel's Paradox again. Man learns from history that man learns nothing from history.*
[74] *Do not think that I have come to destroy (replace) the Law (Torah) or Prophets. I did not come to destroy but to fulfill......Matthew 5, 17.*

So, how are we to understand this writing if all the names have been changed and every cultural scenario is reported OUT of its Torah context? These changes add doubt to the NT account's authenticity regarding both Jesus and his Yeshuaites after his passing; 4) By the end of the first 100 years after Yeshua's passing from the earth, virtually all the NT's original Hebrew writings were translated in the Greek language using the *power* of its abstract terms. Eight hundred years later the Greek NT was Latinized by monks. These theological stories and the term Gospel do not occur in Torah. The *lost in translation* deletions from the NT are the means of getting around an unchangeable Torah; 5) This led the gentile leaders of Shaul's new gospel movement eventually to decree that all the Jewish authors had originally written the letters of the NT in Greek. This claim exists to this day. This is inaccurate. This is what Princes of this world do. It demonstrates how to create a new religion out of an earlier religion: trash the original pristine document by changing concrete terms abstract terms. NT is Yeshua's life counterfeited.

Jesus is not quoted anywhere in the NT scriptures saying that his teachings replace Torah or create a new bible or a new religion. **Torahless** gentiles, using new words from Greek translations enabled that transition. An example: if you read the account of the transfiguration you will see that Yeshua on the spot where all this had just happened, pointedly discouraged his followers from building a worship site and worshiping him or any of the prophets who had been there. In other words, his followers were not to worship nor by implication make a religion of any of the miraculous events just witnessed. Well, has church practice been faithful to this injunction? Obviously not. We should all generalize from Yeshua's simple prohibition. And if we do, we will not trust the Christian NT as we trust Torah. So, *"Depart from me, you workers of Torahlessness."*

Translations of Torah by Hebrews into foreign languages, beginning with the Septuagint in 275 B.C.E. include a side by side copy of the original Hebrew text with each page of the new foreign language translated text. NT translations have not been presented in this clear fashion with the original Aramaic or Hebrew text side by side. Now, you would think the original NT writings would have been carefully guarded to validate various translations. Not so. Fortunately two NT documents in original Hebrew exist in several libraries worldwide: Matthew and Hebrews. Proponents of the NT all start off with "original" Greek. Linguist Nehemiah Gordon reports he found an original Matthew in original Hebrew in the library in Jerusalem. See ***The Hebrew Yeshua v. the Greek Jesus***.

Chapter 10

Glossary of Semitic Words

This glossary[75] includes a sample of the many English biblical words misused today versus their original meanings as they were understood and in use by the nation of Israel 3500 years ago. Using the medium of Torah, the Almighty is able to say what is on His Mind for us. Here are samples of contextual meanings of the Hebrew words chosen by the Almighty to deliver Torah to the nation of Israel at that time: in their own speech *du jour*, in the Hebrew's own linguistic terms. These original meanings are vital for understanding Yehovah's Plans but they are not sustained in current western religious traditions and teachings.

Early, native Canaanites had already been experiencing on some level the presence of God: ݏ ~ **EL** ~ ݏݏݏ ~ **Yehovah**, in their lands for ages, long before the nation of Israel arrived. When Israel went down to Egypt, for famine food and found the Creator as Yehovah, some of them remained in Canaan. They knew the Creator as *El*. Those who left ended up in bondage in Egypt. Some years before 1800 B.C.E. a Canaanite conscript of the Egyptians wrote a prayer on the walls of the cave that was his work site: a turquoise mine in the southern Egyptian Sinai desert. The symbols on those walls are in Paleo Hebrew. He chiseled the symbol for EL written in one stand alone symbol ten times the size of the other symbols. It was in the pictograph of an ox: ݏ, symbolizing great power and the symbol for the Canaanite Creator *El*. **Torah identifies El as *Yehovah***. He asked EL to help him and to not forget him. *Here* he is remembered. This is paleo Hebrew graffiti

---

[75] *A Semitic roots understanding of both biblical and pagan English terms.*

predating the Egyptian plagues, the Exodus of Hebrew slaves from Egypt and Yehovah's Speaking of Torah at Mt. Sinai. A Canaanite turquoise miner or miners, relatives of the nation of Israel worked in the southern Sinai mountains, at Serabit El Khadem and used 22 pictographic symbols borrowed from Egyptian hieroglyphics to represent the consonants in his own spoken language. Approximate date of graffiti is 1853 to 1808 B.C.E. coinciding with the reign of Pharaoh Amenemhet III. It is the earliest known example of Hebrew writing. It demonstrates that some Hebraic workers were there as unwilling laborers. It demonstrates that they knew Yehovah as 𐤀 , the Canaanite's Creator, before they knew His Name. It further links them to Israel. And it provides for God's writing of the Ten Commandments (Ten Words) on the stone tablets in the Hebrew language so that any child who could learn 22 pictorial symbols could also understand the Almighty's words. From these paleo Hebrew beginnings Torah was God given and not man made. **This book gives many examples of human changes to the words of Torah, long after Torah was spoken by Yehovah; The counterfeiting of Torah.**

A guiding literary principle of trust in Yehovah is that one *should* be able to read the entire western bible from Genesis to Revelation in English and have it all make perfect sense. It does not. We look for changes. Identified in this section are some candidates. Everything written after the Torah proper's five scrolls is only commentary on Torah and must fulfill, but not change its descriptions of Yehovah's thinking in the first five. Matthew starts the NT with a counting error in Chapter 1.

א. Aleph: the first letter in the Hebrew and Aramaic aleph beits. 𐤀 is the paleo form. Aleph signifies God, the All Powerful Creator. Aleph also represents the number 1. Each of the 22 symbols represent a letter and a number. Each letter has its own individual pictographic meaning. Modern Hebrew letters (א) do not suggest these meanings. 𐤀 is sounded as *aleph* or *aloof*, meaning the ox, as its great power stands for the Creator. If you take the time to learn these 22 meanings, you will find that your religion has severely limited your understanding of Yehovah's words and His relationship with His people.

Abomination. Synonym *loathing?*, as in a verb made into a noun. This is the Scriptural word so brazenly given to you in the book's title as *Hates*. The word occurs frequently throughout the Tanakh. It characterizes Yehovah's disgust for certain human behaviors. **It causes Him to turn away.** A list of seven things abominable to Yehovah is found in Proverbs 6, 16 to 19. It consists of six behaviors that Yehovah "hates" and they are rhetorically rounded out by a seventh human behavior: inciting quarrels, which elevates the list to abomination status. Were

34,800+ denominations of Christianity developed without quarrels? Not possible. I personally observed a church split as a teenager. I recall the angry quarrels.

America. Why isn't America mentioned in the bible? Yehovah caused the people of His choice to pen the scrolls of the Torah. Churches claim His Authorship also for the NT in their bibles. Very unlikely. Both Torah and NT document ancient events and conversations spoken in the Semitic languages of either Hebrew or Aramaic.[76] As instructed by Torah, observant Jews avoided gentiles: gentiles being peoples of all other civilizations and nations on earth. From Abrams' time (born 2166 B.C.E.) to about 1200 years C.E. no Jewish man cared to know of a civilization in America populated by the aboriginal First Nations tribes of American Indians. In those times there were no foreigners living on the North American continent. While it is certainly true that the Almighty could have referenced America prophetically, He did not. No rock carved petroglyph footprints of family groups have been found in America. Israel did not claim American land with their footprints. The Name יהוה has not been found in the Rocky Mountains or elsewhere on the continent. America is not the land claimed by Yehovah. Why is it so difficult for the American church to understand that this whole thing is not about them? In fact, He could have chosen as His special people the tribes of the Navajo, Sioux, Apache, Algonquin, Seminole, Klamath, Surai, Lakota or Brule. He could have made a covenant to bless them above all other peoples. He could have given them Torah. He chose to bless Abraham's descendant tribes instead. If it turns out that American Indian peoples are genetic descendants of one or more tribes of Israel, then many will realize that the western pop culture of shock and greed has been a poor replacement for the First Nations' cultures of truth and honor. Yehovah's land is located in Canaan.

Some churches have postulated that America is not mentioned because it will not be here due to the *rapture*. This is circular thinking based upon wishful thinking. The plain language of Torah does not describe any human escape pod, nor the church. It doesn't describe any life in the heavenlies. In Torah, the term *heaven* concretely refers to the atmosphere or outer space. Heaven is where Yehovah is, on earth. Everything future for humans happens on earth.

---

[76] *A Jewish man of that era who observed Torah would rather feed his children pork than allow them to learn the pagan language of Greek. As late as 150 C.E. a Greek letter arriving in Jerusalem had to be sent out of the country for translation to Aramaic because no observant Jew living in Jerusalem could read Greek. The only gentile author in Scripture is King Nebuchadnezzar who wrote Daniel 4.*

Anachronism. Literally against the sequence of time; This is where later events in a story are described as being the cause of earlier events! Examples abound and are cited as a reason for faith! Religions use their versions of the NT writings as the foundational story which obsoletes Torah. Hebrew Scriptures become gentile stories. The Western religious world has all this reversed.

Aramaic: also known as Syriac. The Semitic language used in bible times by the people of Israel for everyday living. It came back to Canaan earlier with the return of the Babylonian exiled Hebrew's ancestors, ancient Canaanite tribes. It was in widespread use throughout the Middle East for millennia. Hebrew declined in use by the nation of Israel for the sacred worship of 𐤉𐤄𐤅𐤄. A personal analogy. In the 1960s and 1970s I worshiped in Roman Catholic churches which repeated the liturgy in Latin, except for the homily which was in English. I could understand the Latin spoken there and could repeat many sentences which I had rotely learned. I was not fluent in Latin. I could not write anything new in it. The point is that Greek is not a component part of Jewish biblical history, except for *learned* writers of the Septuagint. An *observant* Jewish man around the start of the common era would rather feed his children pork than allow them to learn Greek. Hebrew for a time became an extinct language except for its use in worship. The Tanakh was written in Hebrew except Daniel 4 included in Daniel 2, 4 all the way to Daniel 7, 28 as well as Ezra 4, 8 to 6, 18 and 7, 12 to 26 which were all written in Syriac. Also written in Aramaic were two words in Genesis 31, 48 and one verse in Jer. 10, 11 and the entire Christian NT. Jesus and his Jewish disciples all spoke native Galilean Aramaic.

Ark, Ark of the Covenant: an acronym for *Aron ha Kodesh* (literally "holy chest"). Noah built a vessel called the ark: Hebrew: *teyvat,* a different word. Noah's ark kept the survivors of a world wide flood disaster. The Aron Ha Kodesh is a vessel in which to keep holy items received from the Almighty. At the front of a Jewish temple sanctuary is the ark for the Torah, a "holy chest" usually containing two or more Torah scrolls. The world's most treasured archaeological object is the Ark of the Covenant which resided in the Holy of Holies in Yehovah's Temple Sanctuary on the Temple Mount in Jerusalem. The Presence of Yehovah resided in the Ark of the Covenant. It also contained the tablets of the Ten Words, Aaron's staff and manna. The instructions for building the Ark of the Covenant and the Temple are found in the Torah excruciatingly exact in all respects. Yehovah says in Torah that the Temple was built by King Schlomo to Yehovah's detailed instructions as a mirror of Yehovah's throne room in Yehovah's heavenly dimension. In Torah, little information is given about heaven, however the ancient mystical Hebrew writings known as Kabbala describe seven levels of heaven with some very interesting implications.

Nebuchadnezzar, king of Babylon (Iraq) sent the commander of his armed forces (Nebuzara dan) to plunder Jerusalem of the Ark of the Covenant in 586 B.C.E.. In 585 he walked into an empty Holy of Holies. King Schlomo, using technology obtained from the Egyptians by marrying into Pharoah's family (I Kings 5, 10) built the Temple using a sand hydraulic elevator under the Ark in the Holy of Holies. Hiram of Tyre, another Hiram, not the king, constructed two huge but precision molded hollow columns cast from molten brass.[77] Hiram's father was a skilled craftsman in bronze and his mother was of the Hebrew tribe of Naphtali. The two columns were placed in the door of the porch in front of the door of the House of Yehovah. The hollow pillar columns acted as elevated sand reservoirs hidden and also aided by heavy bronze capitals placed on top of and inserted *into* the columns. In I Kings 7, 15 to 21 and through 47 the dimensions of the columns are 18 cubits high and 12 cubits in circumference; The right is named *Jachin* and the left pillar *Boaz* (reported to be Hebrew words for lever and fulcrum, not personally checked). The capitals are reported at time of construction to be **5 cubits high** while installed. There is a secret society in America developed from this episode of Hiram's work of casting temple columns. The existence of the sand elevator is the secret. In one of their buildings one can see *Jachin* and *Boaz* displayed prominently. Masons.

Here's the point of this: in II Kings 25, 17 *after* Nebuzara dan destroyed the Jerusalem Temple and its walls, the pillars are still 18 cubits in height but now the brass capitals are only **3 cubits high**. Two cubits (36 inches) shorter. The Ark sat on an elevator with a long lever running to the fulcrum so that it could be dropped 18 feet or so. The reverse of a normal lever fulcrum arrangement, it used the very heavy weight of the capitals and sand as leverage dropping a short vertical height of only two cubits in order to move a lighter weight (the elevator platform) a longer vertical height (12 cubits). After the Ark was removed from the bottom elevator floor, loss of sand in the second hollow column pillar raised the empty elevator back up to the Temple floor and lowered the second capital to its final 3 cubit resting height alongside its twin. This system allowed the Ark to be stealthily removed for safekeeping through the catacombs of Solomon's limestone quarry under the Temple Mount. The Babylonian siege of Jerusalem lasted about a year. A vast network of underground caves is accessed today via the entrance to Zedekiah's cave. It stretches from Solomon's quarry all the way to Jericho. Hiding places for the Ark are likely

---

[77]*Hiram cast them in the clay ground in Kakar in the plain of Jericho beside the Jordan River between Succoth and Zarthan. I Kings 7, 46.*

infinite in number. Nebuchadnezzar's general conquered Jerusalem but entered the Sanctuary of the House of God in Jerusalem's Temple to find it empty. Today, on the rock floor of the foundation on the Temple Mount there can be seen the four unlocking staves which activated the elevator. The second priest and the three keepers of the door stood on the four staves to activate the elevator mechanism. These details from Michael Rood. Sadly, American clergy has been too quick to criticize King Solomon's *sinful* behavior in becoming Pharaoh's son in law. The sand hydraulics technology was a family secret of Pharaoh, King of Egypt. Solomon married for the technology. I believe people who say that the Ark is safe in Israel, but only Yehovah knows where.

A contract has been put out by the modern equivalent of the Sanhedrin for a quickly constructed temporary building which is exact in its dimensions to the Temple. They have the sacrificial altar. They have the correct breed of red bovine critter for the sacrifices and await only the birth of a blemish free specimen, an occurrence totally up to Yehovah's timing. With some difficulty they have *almost* reproduced the menorah in gold in its original dimensions. Gold is a heavy but soft metal. When long arms are built of it, eight feet long, it has trouble holding up its own weight, unless it is not pure gold. So the stage is set and earth awaits Yehovah's chronology. Presently we see the desolation of the Temple site on the Temple Mount as the current Palestinian Muslim occupants have leveled it down to its foundation stones and have erected two mosques (one is the Dome of the Rock) built on the Temple foundation stones. Yehovah's own Sanctuary has been made desolate by foreigners. This book points out that foreign religions on His Land and in this case on His very SANCTUARY is an *abomination* to Him: The Dome of the Rock does not cover the precise location of the Temple Holy of Holies which is elsewhere.

Believer. Christians use this term to refer to those who recognize Jesus as their Savior. Modern believers do not observe a Torah lifestyle.[78] Jesus' talmadim were headquartered in Israel from the time of Jesus' passing from earth to the destruction of Jerusalem and the temple, a period of 40 years. They differed from all other Hebrews in *only one* respect: they believed that Yeshua was the Messiah. The Christian NT excludes almost all Hebraic details of these Messianic believers during these 40 years; This is not intellectually tolerable considering that these were the only believers who as were EYEWITNESSES to Yeshua and to his teachings. From

---

[78] *Circumcised, observe the Sabbath and the three spring feasts and three fall feasts of YHWH via lunar calendar; worship Yahweh by Sh'ma. Wear tsi tsi. Keep Torah of Moshe; shun teachings of ancient rabbis and foreigners.* **Eat the meal on Passover.**

all sources, we know that these "Judeo Christians", here called Yeshuaites, duplicated Jesus teachings by observing Torah of Moshe. How did the NT omit their Torah observant activities? The NT's subsequent Greek translations obscured, after the fact, that Yeshua himself was obedient to Torah. The NT book of Acts is a historical setup. It's a fictional rewrite of history; The NT replaced Yeshua's teachings of Torah observance with a new persistent theme of *faith*. It is a themed false rendering of the original Hebrew first five books of NT. If one carefully reads Yeshua's quotes of Torah in the NT's first five, we find that there is evidence left showing his obedience to Torah. For example, Yeshua reiterated that the Shema is the greatest commandment and in so doing affirmed that all his followers should worship Yehovah who is One and He alone is God, monotheism. The word *believer* is a poor substitute for *observant*. Jesus was not a believer who preached Gospel, but he was observant of Torah. Even Ha Satan believes but is not Torah observant. Every word, every idea found in the NT should spring only from ancient Torah. It is not enough to believe Torah, Yeshua's teaching was to *observe* Yehovah's Sayings. As a result believers disrespect Yehovah by substituting the Savior Jesus for the Savior Yehovah and replace Yehovah's Passover with Constantine's Easter.

    B.C.E. *Before the Common Era.* The first Temple in Jerusalem was destroyed in 586 B.C.E. The second temple was started in 538 B.C.E. and destroyed in 70 CE (*common era*). Hebrews do not recognize Jesus Christ as God nor as Messiah, so a calendar based on the year of his birth is not acceptable to them. Ironically, many Hebrews have noted that in the western calendar, the birth of Yeshua occurred in the year 4 B.C.E. We might say the Hebrews are historically accurate about their own history, while western Christianity has trouble counting: their Sabbath is the first day, not the seventh; Good Friday to Easter Sunday is not three days and three nights; and now starting a calendar by replacing zero with minus four.

    Canaan. The pre Israelite land promised by Yehovah to Abraham's descendants. The Canaanites include blood relatives of Abraham's descendants who were aware of the Almighty whom they worshiped variously as ﭏ , EL, Elohim before Torah. Some were uncles to the tribes of Israel who went down to Egypt.

    Christian. A pagan term (see pagan, it's not what you think) approximately derived from the Greek English *christos*. *Christos* and Messiah are not equivalent. The Greeks were polytheistic worshipers who knew many christs. Jesus the christ was just one of them. If you call yourself a Christian you are continuing a human tradition of renaming Yeshua ben Yosef with a pagan word relegating him to co status with other Greek pagan mythological gods believed by the Greeks to be deities. Deuteronomy 12, 29 to 31: [*Do not find out how other nations worship their gods and then adopt their customs for the worship of Yehovah; For everything that is an abomination to Yehovah, which He hates, these nations have done to their gods.* Don't turn around and do these things for Me and call them Holy as if you are doing them for My sake.] By even calling yourself a Christian you are doing what Yehovah says in Deuteronomy 12 not to do. In the same way, Christian teachings after Yeshua died, elevated Jesus to the status of God. This is a human created foreign religion, which worships the created not the Creator. It is *another religion*.

Church. A pagan addition to Semitic scriptures. It does not appear in the Scriptures: not in Torah, Writings nor Prophets; Not even in the NT! The Semitic word in English is *assembly* or *gathering* as in family gathering. "Do not forsake the gathering of yourselves together" means do not refrain from gathering your family in your tent on the Sabbath to worship Yehovah.

Damascus, Syria is the oldest continuously inhabited city on earth. Shaul (Paul) claimed a conversion near Damascus. Yehovah has plans for Damascus and they are not good. Isaiah 17,1 tells us that Damascus will become a smoking black hole in the ground. There are other long pending and as yet unfulfilled prophecies from other Tanakh sources such as Zechariah's flying scrolls and the seven layers of Daniel's prophecies. In concert with these, we can expect the next big prophetic event on Yehovah's calendar to be the total destruction of Damascus, Syria. As of this writing the current President of Iran, Amenabinajad lives not in Iran, but in Damascus, Syria.

Doctrine. Refers not to abstract principles but to the basic rules by which a person chooses to live his life. It is a down to earth, concrete, habitual lifestyle: it is behavior. Yeshua's doctrine was Torah. A lowly shepherd or an seven year old child can understand it. On the other hand, religions use *doctrine* to refer to explanations of complex and intricate systems of beliefs about abstract issues which are not completely understood except by the highly educated. Because of the level of sophistication of these doctrines, each church has a highly trained Seminary graduate to lead them. In other words, the doctrines of Torah observance are understood by an seven year old, but the church doctrines require a full 20 years of formal academic education. Doctrine, to the religious is man made abstract polemic dogma.

Earth or World. One Hebrew word is *eretz* meaning land. There are other words for earth or world but when *eretz* is used it almost always refers to the land of Israel not to the entire planet. Rethink what you have been taught about the "Great Commission" which uses *eretz*. In other words the passage should read, [**Go into all**

the land of Israel teaching My people to return to Torah as I have taught you.]

Elohim. A term for the Creator from the Canaanites, who preceded Israel in the promised land. Literally, it can mean God, gods and judges. It is a usage which God allowed for a period of time until He revealed His true Name to the nation of Israel. It is still used. The three meanings are used in the Semitic text as a pun in Psalm 82 where Yeshua uses Yehovah's Tanakh statement [I have said you people are Elohim] to cleverly once again refer to himself inferentially as a son of man (See Matthew 16, 14 to 20 and Luke 24, 44 to 53.) Colloquially, *Elohim* means "our God" referring to the One and only living God of Israel.

Exemplar or ensample. A physical object left over as a sign of the personal intervention of Yehovah into human history. A concrete example which requires no faith whatsoever to understand. Thus it is capable of being understood by a seven year old child and is not subject to interpretation by self appointed messengers from God. For example I have in my possession one piece of leftover brimstone picked up from among the millions of pieces strewn about the ruins of Sodom, Gomorrah, Zebulin and Admah in the desert just east of the Dead Sea. To educate yourself and gain a new respect for the power of the Almighty as well as the authenticity of Torah, you should view DVDs available from Michael Rood one of which shows the ruins of Sodom and Gomorrah. People love to explain how all this is just part of the natural phenomena of various physical science systems at work; But they miss the point that on the site there is still the evidence that Torah's details of the destruction are true. Another exemplar is the coral encrusted remains of Pharoah's army of chariots over a mile and a half of the floor of the crossing site of the Yom Suf when Israel fled Egypt and crossed over on dry land. Six hundred years later, King Solomon placed two columns marking each side of the crossing site as Torah ordered. Torah says Pharaoh perished there with his army. I have underwater video which clearly shows all of this as well as the four spoked wheel of gold on Pharoah's personal chariot. Hebrew leaders retrieved the wheel and it is safe in Israel. As mentioned above, the Ark of the Covenant still resides in the land of Israel. It contains a portion of manna, the staff of Aaron that blossomed and the stone tablets upon which Yehovah wrote the Ten Words with His finger. When Yehovah decides these exemplars are ready to be revealed for the entire world to experience, many will return to Torah. You could return now.

Karaite. Also *Scripturalist*. A sect of Judaism which believes only in the written Torah of Moshe with no changes, no additions or subtractions. It is the original Way of Torah practiced by the nation 3,500 years ago. Karaites say individual interpretations of Scripture are allowable as long as one has not changed

Torah. They do not tolerate irrational interpretations which change Scripture. They do not accept a second oral Torah handed down to the rabbis orally from Moshe, nor the post biblical writings of Torah derivative religions such as Christianity. The current name for them, Karaites, dates from about the 800s B.C.E. or before the Middle Ages. Karaites join other forms of Judaism saying this about Messiah: When Messiah comes there will be peace on earth. Is there peace on earth? NO. Therefore, Messiah has not yet come. Therefore Yeshua at this point in time is not viewed by Karaites as Messiah. See Land, Messiah.

Faith. In the Hebrew bible, the ancient word means *trust* in the Torah Ways of God. In the NT *faith* in Salvation and the many other theological constructs replaces Torah observance. Biblical trust refers to the Words and Ways of Yehovah, not belief in theological constructs, the thinking of man. As antiquity's finds and Torah based Hebrew traditions concretely show the truth of Torah's record, less and less faith is needed to believe the Torah record of events. But theological concepts are not subject to concrete verification, thus faith *is* required.

Fiddle. The practice of making a Torah proscription more intellectually ergonomic in the minds of those feeling bound by the irritating prohibitive torah.

God. In this book we prefer *Yehovah* to pronounce the Name spelled as *yod hei vav hei*. We also freely use *Almighty, Creator, El, Elohim, God* and *Yahweh* to refer to The Creator. Use of any of these words would be sufficient to convict us if we were to swear by any of them and testify falsely under oath in civil court.

Gentile. Anyone who is not genetically a member one of the thirteen tribes of Israel through the lineage of Abraham, Isaac and Jacob. Anyone who is not a Jew. Foreigners living in Israel are charitably called *B'nai Noach:* Children of Noah. For contrast see *pagan*. But, Yehovah calls gentile *sojourners* "My gentiles".

Grace. A term used sparingly in the Tanakh but frequently in the NT. The concept of grace from the Christian NT is used by Christians to justify not observing Torah. A popular saying is " *We are not under the Law. Jesus sacrificed himself and did away with all that. We are free from the Law because we are under Grace.*" One biblical ding on that thinking is found in the Tanakh in I Samuel 15, 22 where Yehovah says that He takes more pleasure in His people following His Ways as spoken in Torah than in either burnt offerings or sacrifices. There is the statement that Noah found **grace in the eyes** of the Almighty long BEFORE Yeshua's time. The Hebrew word *gracious* refers to God's Eyes shining with happiness. Noah pleased God by personally adopting His Ways. The fact of Grace from God began not as a theory, but as a personality attribute God exhibits when He considers someone who follows His Ways. It makes His Eyes light up. The ancient patriarchs knew El Shaddai's Ways and it enabled them to please the Almighty before Moshe was given Torah and thousands of years before Yeshua. Yehovah's Sayings and the example of the patriarchs demonstrate that observing Torah leads to knowing and understanding God. It is not a theological construct, it's a divine *personal* attribute.

Holy. From the mind and words of the Almighty, Yehovah.

Ha Shem: literally, "the name". Reading Genesis 1, 1 in an English rabbinic sourced bible one finds this: *In the beginning, the name created the heavens and the earth...* In Judaism the Name of God is not written. It is spoken aloud only in rituals. They offer compelling reasons for this practice due to the need to reconcile two apparently conflicting torahs regarding God's name. Foreigners, ignorant of Torah should not criticize them.

Hebrew. The Semitic language the Almighty used to provide His Torah to the thirteen tribes of Israel for their use in worship of Him; A set apart language. Nowadays also the native Hebrew speakers. Torah was initially written in Paleo Hebrew. Paleo Hebrew used scribed pictographic letters symbolic of concrete objects such an ox, a window, a head, etc. Each object's name is the three consonants of the word from its sound spoken aloud. The shape of these Hebrew aleph beit symbols have gone through a number of changes throughout the nation's history, including times of exile from the land. The modern symbols no longer intrinsically evoke the original pictographic meanings. However, the original identity and the symbolic meaning of each letter, which stands for the sounds of 22 consonants in spoken Hebrew, have not changed with these iterations of form. For every day use, the people in Yeshua's location spoke the Galilean dialect of Aramaic (Syriac). It was their native language. There is no Torah reason why important Holy Land events spoken in an everyday language (Aramaic) and written down in that language as well as the divine language (Hebrew) would need to be translated into a non Semitic language (Greek) in order to authenticate the events in the life of first century Yeshuaites living in the land. See **House of Israel** for more evidence for this assertion. From historical sources we know that observant Hebrews shunned the Greek language. The Christian teaching is that Greek translations allowed the Gospel to be spread throughout the rest of the world. **That order, the Great Commission of Yeshua only exists in the later Greek version of the NT.** It's circular. The G.C. actually is alien to the Judaic teachings of Yeshua. The first century Semitic description of future events from the NT says that spreading of a worldwide revival will be done by 12,000 evangelists from each of the thirteen tribes of Israel. Yeshua directed his talmadim to continue his teaching of Torah to Jews first and then to

Torah loving gentiles living throughout the land of Big Israel. He said that he had come only for the lost House of Israel referring to the ten tribes of northern Judah. There is no direct reference to the rest of the planet, nor to nonTorah loving gentiles. Christian teachings anachronistically and incorrectly lumped in later scripture from Revelation where 144,000 Hebrew evangelists spread throughout the planet. Early survivors of Yeshua obeyed him in this regard sticking to *Eretz Israel*; Then, Christians began using a changed version of Yeshua's teachings and started planet wide *gentile* evangelical missions.

House of Israel: refers to the ten tribes north of Judah, the Northern Kingdom, the northern tribes or house of Israel. Beginning with the division of King David and King Solomon's united kingdom, Jereboam, Solomon's administrator led the ten tribes in revolt. Also called the "lost tribes". It is doubtful that Yehovah has lost them. Rather the ten northern tribes are lost to the land of Israel and because they were assimilated into other nations their Jewish identity is lessened. They are symbolized by the tribe of Ephraim. Y'huda (Judah) is symbolic of the two southern tribes who are the historic Jews who have inhabited the Land of Israel for a very long period of time. See **Judaism** for Y'huda's role in the beginnings of Judaism, the religion. (The linguistic root of the word Jew is the word Judah.) One function of Messiah is to restore all thirteen tribes to the land of Israel. **Read the bones chapter of Ezekial 37 with this in mind.** Yeshua was asked by a Phoenician woman, a gentile, to spread his blessings around to encompass her gentiles. He responded that he had come only for the lost house of Israel.[79] He clearly points out that he has **not come to teach gentiles**. His words should be a huge wake up call for Christians.

Israel: not house of, is the man formerly named Jacob, Ya'akov. Yisrael refers to the promised land. This encompasses the land from the Nile river to the Euphrates river where the feet of Israelites walked while leaving Egypt and following God's cloud forty years through the deserts of the Middle East. It includes parts of Egypt, all of present day Israel, Jordan, Syria, Lebanon and Saudi Arabia. See Deuteronomy 1, verses 2 and 3. Israel, *big Israel,* is vastly larger than what we see on modern maps as the tiny *country* of Israel. Three hundred thousand square miles versus thirty thousand square miles. Eretz Israel is huge. The Almighty's claim is on all this land. Any person or group who alliances themselves against Yehovah's purposes for His land will find themselves rowing against the certain tide of His will. This does not mean that Israel the nation will occupy all the land of Israel. Descendants of Esau living in Se'ir (Deuteronomy 2, 4) and of Lot living in Moav

---

[79] *Is he the gentile Savior? Matt. 15, 21to 24.*

(Deuteronomy 2, 9) have their own lands allotted to them by Yehovah. Where does America stand in all this? Nowhere. The Almighty told Abraham that the Promised Land would include all the land upon which the feet of the people of the nation of Israel TROD UPON while crossing the desert. Interestingly, the people took this to heart and carved petroglyphs in the likenesses of the footprints of their family members in the rocks of the desert wherever they traveled. Three or four pairs of footprints: a pair of big feet, a pair of middle sized feet and pairs of little feet. All lined up next to each other: sandal prints carved in stone. There are millions of footprint petroglyphs all over the desert lands from the Nile river to the Euphrates and going east from the Mediterranean sea. None have been found in America. Yehovah was real to them.

Israel, Tzion or Zion also refers to the Israelites or children of the man Israel and the nation of Israel dwelling in *eretz Israel*. For Jewish people this term *Israelite* has negative connotations from misuse by the western Christian world, therefore many Hebrews avoid its usage. This is a legacy from the false Christian teaching of the Theory of Replacement: which says Israelites have just fouled up one too many times and the Almighty has replaced them with born again Christians who are now His chosen people. On its face, this is blatantly anti Semitic. For messianic believers, the Israelites are instead REVERED as the chosen people who in the future will be their teachers and priests.[80] As just noted a couple paragraphs ago replacement theory ignores Yeshua's stated purpose for his ministry: to return the lost House of Israel to Torah observance.

Judaism. Foreigners should not look down their noses at Judaism, the religion. The temple is Yehovah's sanctuary on earth. When it was destroyed in 586 B.C.E., the nation of Israel lost its national place of worship, but they still had the Torah. They began meeting in small groups to study Torah, as national worship was reduced to individual action. These assemblies became "synagogues". After the rebuilding of the temple around 520 to 515 B.C.E., synagogues continued to play a role in making Torah become part of the people's hearts. This synagogue life became the religious practice of Judaism as opposed to temple life the nation of Israel originally practiced by Torah. However, Yeshua frequented synagogues and his brother James had one in his Yeshuaite complex after Yeshua's passing. In both cases, the teaching was designed to bring the people back to written Torah of Moshe.

---

[80] *See Our Hands are Stained with His Blood (chapter 12) and The Race to Save the World. Also The Big Lie of Replacement Theory, a teaching of Jonathon Bernis.*

Two hundred years later, the Mishna (written oral law) was scribed with the Talmud (Heb. "to learn") along with the Gemara (commentary on the Mishna). The roots of the Talmud are the ancient rabbis' commentary on how dispersed Jews should apply written Torah while not living in the land of Israel and for a nation unable to worship in the Temple. Who are we ignorant foreigners that we should judge them?

Land. In Hebrew the word is *eretz*, an essential word to have translated from a Hebraic perspective in that it almost always refers to the land of Israel, not the entire earth. All of the special circumstances of blessings related to land which one finds in a quick reading of the Torah refer to the Land of Israel. Corruption of the word *eretz* has enabled the pagan concept dubbed the Great Commission of Jesus which so defines the misguided missionary activities of gentile Christians. The phrase "go into all the world" means go into all of the land of Israel. In the Great Commission the talmidim of Yeshua were told to spread his message of obedience to Torah to the ten lost tribes of the house of Israel, throughout all the land of Israel. This is a far cry from what has actually happened, isn't it? The land of Israel is sacred to the Almighty. He has the big plan of ultimately residing there with His people. All of the events written in Torah are centered in the land of Israel.[81] There is no provision for offering sacrifice with the produce of other lands. Is your income derived from production in Israel's land? If not, rethink your participation in Gentile Tithing Schemes.

Yehovah's Presence dwelled upon this earth for perhaps a half millennium. He is coming back to **His land eretz Israel**. The Christian teaching of the Second Coming substitutes the return of Jesus for the return of Yehovah. This is difficult to follow since the Church's NT calls both of them "Lord". The messianic belief is that after Yehovah's agent, Messiah, has made peace on earth, then He, Yehovah, will dwell on earth with His people in the land of Israel. Everything centers on the land of Israel. Yehovah speaks of His land as His own **Inheritance**.

Law. THE most poorly translated word in the gentile scriptures. When used in the Latinized Greek based scriptures it appears in the place of God's Semitic term Torah. It is so broad a term that any speaker can make it refer to whatever he likes. This is how people created a new religion and con others around them into thinking *their* way. By one word change, humans twisted Torah around to be the new indictment (law) of all who fail to follow new traditions (NTs?) declared by the same men to be HOLY. It's usage is so broad and vague that the term really is devoid of

---

[81] *Deuteronomy 11, 12. God cares for eretz Israel, he looks at it every day.*

meaning. *Torah* comes from the root word *yorah* which means teach. This supports the view that Yeshua is *Torah* **teacher** in the flesh. Get it? Jesus was the teach. He taught Torah; His ministry fulfilled Torah. In place of *Law's* vagueness, Torah refers to a single well defined object: the written scrolls of Moses: the first five books of the bible. The Ten Words were written in stone tablets by the finger of 𐤉𐤄𐤅𐤄. **The Ten Words apply the ancient Ways of Yehovah to everyone**. Yeshua claimed to be the fulfillment of Torah. He was Torah in the flesh. His teaching goals were to bring Yisrael back to Torah. He died in that attempt. He died for Torah. Torah is the Way noted in Scriptures. The word Law means none of these things. The vague ideas that the word *law* refers to are in fact unScriptural, pagan beliefs. Don't use the word law, use Torah, the word that Yeshua and Yehovah use.

Lord. Right behind *Law* as the second worst translated term in the English bible. It is a term arising in the King James English Version of the bible. Over the last one thousand years or so, any landed gentry in Great Britain have been given the socieo economic title *Lord*. Why should the Almighty be given a pagan class ridden, British gentrified title? The historically accurate Name of God in the ancient Hebrew literature is Yehovah > יהוה > 𐤉𐤄𐤅𐤄 > 𐤋. In the place of *lord*, another term could have been chosen to represent the Almighty's name. It already appears in Scripture. It has the same referenced meaning of master or owner and is a Hebrew word, but it has a pagan origin. The term is *ba'al*. Ba'al was the Canaanite storm god. Take some time to substitute the word *ba'al* for the word *lord* sometime in your devotions and see how you like the accompanying feeling of abomination. This suggestion was for wake up value only. Do not dwell on this practice.

In the Christian world the term Lord is used to refer both to the Almighty or the man Yeshua without distinction. This tradition made holy by men muddies the distinction between Yehovah and Yeshua. The first individual to know the personal Name of the Almighty according to Scripture is Moshe. "*I am Yehovah. I appeared to Abraham, to Isaac, and to Jacob, as EL shaddai. But by My Name Yehovah was I not known to them.*" Contrast this important piece of information with the diverse numbers of pagan names that **Torahless** peoples of the earth have thought up for the Almighty. It is still true today that almost no one on earth proclaims the Name of Yehovah, including the people of Judaism and Christianity. There is only one Yehovah. Saying, " Jesus is Lord" is as unScriptural as saying , "Jesus is ba'al". In Exodus 3, 13 to 15 Yehovah states what His Name is to be for all eternity. From the *Complete Jewish Bible*:

"Moshe said to God, Look, when I appear before the people of Israel and say to them, The God of your ancestors has sent me to you; and they ask me, What

is his name? What am I to tell them? God said to Moshe, "Ehyeh Asher Ehyehh " [I am what I am, or I WILL BE WHAT I WILL BE], and He added, "This is what you will say to the people of Israel: Ehyeh has sent me to you." God said further to Moshe, " Say this to the people of Israel: yod hei vav hei [Yehovah, Yehovah], the God of your fathers, the God of Avraham, the God of Yitz'chak, the God of Ya'akov, has sent me to you. This is my name forever; this is how I am to be remembered generation after generation".

"*This is my name forever; this is how I am to be remembered generation after generation*". Few remember to use His Name *Yehovah*. Therefore we point out again that God Hates Religion.

Marriage: For several years author and wife taught Marriage Ministries, International group courses. Based upon that experience, present day expectations differ significantly from the teachings of Torah and Jesus. In ancient times if you were having sex with a woman, you were married to her *in the Eyes of Yehovah*. Torah marriage customs are a fine example of a life event that *was* minimally complex yet provided safeguards for the less privileged: a Torah theme and in this case for the wife. In the Hebrew's ancient culture, which was good enough to provide racial immortality before Yehovah, a marriage "ceremony" involved the man going to her father's abode and bringing her and her belongings back with him to his abode. He and her father may have exchanged a sandal or some other agreed upon action and that was it. No marriage ceremony. If the Almighty was not happy with the Hebrew's marital customs, He could have made Torah changes to it. In those days, marriage was also not a societal institution. It was not at all what we think of today. It was not eternal and not always lifelong! If a man so married began having sex with another woman, Jesus taught that he should follow Torah, *be a man*, realize he cannot have them both, take responsibility and not let it drag on but leave his wife by exercising a bill of divorcement so that she can get on with her life. It's a forced choice, a torah known by everyone. This practical arrangement was congruent with the ancient ways of Yehovah and good enough for Yeshua to advocate a return to Torah, but not for modern western religion which views marriage as a sacred *institution, an underpinning of civilized society*. Modern marriage traditions of men declare something holy that the Almighty has not. The modern religious dismiss Yehovah's ancient ways of the marriage as outmoded, declaring Marriage a Holy institution. Has that worked out better? Certainly for the Economy, which is cranked up with lawyer's fees and real estate transactions. Modern life in general is very complicated, a consequence of Torahless modern civil authorities creating a society of Torahless "holy" conventions. Your parents were married in Yehovah's mind even if never officially married in the pagan (Torahless) traditions of civil or religious authorities. Therefore **do not harbor thoughts of being illegitimate.**

Messiah: from the word MSH or the letters *mem*, *shin*, *chet* ~ M SH CH: filled in vowels = *Ma* **Shi** *ach* To paint, smear or anoint as with oil. Literally, "anointed one". This refers to Abraham, Isaac, Jacob, Moshe, Aaron, David and all the prophets, kings of both kingdoms, King Cyrus of Persia, Yeshua and *anyone else* that Yehovah may appoint as His Mashiach in the future. It should be obvious that messiahs are not God. The concept of Messiah is not found in Torah proper and not explicitly found even in the great prophetic scroll of Isaiah! In Isaiah 2, 4 there is a reference to *Olam Haba* which means *world to come*. Scriptures say Messiah will: 1) Return all tribes to the land of Israel; 2) Restore Jerusalem; 3) Establish a one world government with its center in the land of Israel; 4) Rebuild the Temple and restore Temple worship; and 5) Establish Torah as the doctrine of the land to include the religious court system of Israel.

During the first 500 or so years after the giving of Torah there was no law enforcement system or official government judges with bailiffs, jails, prosecutors, attorneys, juries, jury consultants, armed guards, etc. While Yehovah's Presence was dwelling with Israel, there was only the accused, the Priest and Torah. Torah was the only doctrine of the land of Israel. The effect of Messiah from our standpoint will be to institute world wide peace by exchanging the world's religions for Torah and Yehovah's ancient Ways. The fact is that none of these five functions of Messiah have occurred yet. All who have claimed to be Messiah have died without accomplishing any of these goals. Thus Jesus by all accounts is *presently* not Messiah. The future is Yehovah's. You do realize that many biblical prophecies have yet to come into fulfillment on this earth, right? Presently it could be about 50%.

The historical person whose real name is Yeshua ben Yosef is nowhere quoted in the NT as claiming himself to be Messiah! He often called himself a servant of his Father. He often called himself by the phrase "son of man". That phrase is the one that Yehovah used when talking to his prophets such as Ezekial as noted elsewhere. Jesus is the biblically the latest of Yehovah's anointed ones, His prophets. A Hebrew word for him is *Moshiach* (from James Tabor's *Restoring Abrahamic Faith*). It is a long tortured stretch from *son of man* to Son of God, a title which Yeshua never claimed for himself. Only *other persons* claimed it for him, including some accusatory rabbinic leaders, and other evil (Torah breakers) men, of the day! Your Christian NT is not the infallible word of God. The NT was spoken and written down in Aramaic. Unless your NT is translated from all Aramaic sources or comes from the Yeshuaites, it has been paganized. Yeshua lived the life of a prophet within the Torah confines of a kosher rabbi . He taught the people of Israel and existing sects of Judaism restoration to Torah, *res TORAH ation*. In fact he called himself the fulfillment of Torah. Rather than being God, he was Torah in the flesh. When he says, I am this or I am that, he is saying Torah is this and Torah is that. In the gospel of John this is the real meaning of the term Word, i.e. Torah, and it is describing Torah in the flesh. Nowadays, theological teachings have gone looping off into pagan underbrush claiming attributes of the Greek term LOGOS. Isaiah does not even prophesy messiah. Instead he prophesies Yehovah alone ruling over the entire world. Messiah's role was developed centuries later. Understood in the context of the Hebrew Tanakh, which is the "Bible" Yeshua quoted, Yeshua sacrificed his life for Yehovah's written Ways and therefore we say that he died in its defense.

Midian: as in the land of Midian: this is Saudi Arabia. Mount Sinai is in the land of Midian, not in Egypt. The Saudi royalty have been shown Mt. Sinai by a petroleum engineer, the amateur archaeologist who discovered it identified by all the surrounding features as described in Torah events. He documented its features over a period of years and under duress pointed it all out to them by helicopter. **Mount Sinai is now fenced off with armed security guards.** See Michael Rood's videos.

Minister: or *Pastor* is found Semitically only two or three times in the NT. The Semitic term for elder is found dozens of times. This implies that in NT times elders ran the "churches" but nowadays ministers have control. Ministers counter that their authority derives from the prolific NT and Tanakh term *messenger*. Torturing a Torah term to benefit one class of persons creates a host of problems not the least of which is the proliferation of ✞ sects and denominations (in excess of 34,800+). Denominations is a crafted term for Names. It gives a **name** to what would otherwise be the value *number* of a currency bill. Can you imagine a Torah scroll titled Names? Nope. There is only one Name in Torah, Yehovah. Relative to human beings there *is* a scroll identified as Numbers, indicating we all on the same level playing field. Denominational *names* offers a way around this fundamental reality of Yehovah's creation. For Hebrews everyone else is below that Name, part of numbered tribe, equally subject to Torah and all on the same level playing field, *even* the priests. Ministers or pastors derive their authority from their Denomination and are a substitution or *reenactment* of Yehovah's priests. The priests' authority derives from Yehovah's choice based upon genetics (Aaron). Too many self proclaimed "messengers" in Christendom routinely exploit their human endowed ministerial teaching authority.[82] It is common for ministers in the Christian church to usurp the authority of a father in his own house. There should be no one between a family's father and Yehovah. However, **few gentile fathers know Torah**. By design, their church has failed to teach it to them. The existence of Church denominations implies that each elevates itself above the others, up higher, towards the Almighty's name. But even in today's pagan world there are ministers who are truly beautiful people, but operating in a corrupted Torah deficient system.

Mikvah. The Hebrew word for a ritual, healing bath. In addition to its hygienic function, it is symbolic of an individual's desire to prepare to ask for forgiveness (reunite with Israel) in God's sanctioned lifestyle which is observing the Torah Ways of Yehovah. This lifestyle is our personal sanctuary. If you break Torah, then *you* may trigger your reunion with Israel with a *mitzvah*. So unless you are otherwise ill, the longest you have to wait "unclean" is until that evening. See Leviticus 15, realizing that many torahs only apply to the priestly tribe. If you avoid mitzvah and have gone back to your old pagan religious ways of sin and guilt you will be waiting longer. The NT plan of salvation is a pagan change to Torah's provision for reuniting with Israel via *mikvah* plus offerings and the national Day of Atonement. This definition is an incomplete simplification of biblical forgiveness, as nowadays we are living with no Presence Of Yehovah in Israel, no Temple, and no organized priesthood of Aaron.

Nephilim. The Hebrew word in Genesis 6,4 is mistranslated as *giants*: "In those days there were giants in the land". Nephilim means subhuman creatures. Lower than human but closer to humans than to chimpanzees, like the Neanderthals who were very skilled flint tool makers and contribute up to about 5 % of modern homo sapiens genetics, depending upon geography of ancestors. Africans have none. It contributes disease resistance. See *nephilim* discussion on page 29.

New Covenant. In Jeremiah 31, 31 to 33 Yehovah says that the days are coming when He will make a new covenant with the house of Israel and with the house of Judah. At that time what role would *faith* fulfill?

"I will put My Torah within them and write it on their hearts; I will be their God, and they will be My people. No longer will any of them teach his fellow community member or his brother, 'Know Adonai'; for all will know me, from the least of them to the greatest." (CJB).

There will be no churches, no need for teaching the Righteous about God. New

---

[82] *Zechariah 14 describes Yahweh ruling alone over the whole planet. The messenger is of His Face. A Messiah is not mentioned. Everyone will know and worship Him and keep the Feast of Tabernacles. Teaching will be obsolete.*

covenant refers to Torah written on hearts. Yeshua had Torah written upon his heart. The NT scriptures erroneously redirect this prophetic blessing to designate the believers of Jesus as the new replacement for Hebrews, receivers of Yehovah's blessings who live pagan derived theoretical doctrines which reject Torah! This theology is false witness of Yehovah's Ways. Hebrew 8 year olds understand spoken Torah with little explanation. Theological precepts, in contrast require years of postgraduate study by adults relying heavily upon mature human formal thinking operations.

NT is this book's abbreviation for "New Testament" or the second half of the Christian bible. Those two words imply that Torah, the first half of foreigners' bibles, is old, outdated and replaced with the NT's *new* information.. So, NT is all you are getting out of me. Yehovah's Words say the opposite: His Words, His Information, cannot be changed, no matter what. NT, the words, is an anti Semitic and unacceptable title for personal letters incompletely describing the events surrounding the life of Yeshua ben Yosef. The NT's Semitic four gospel letter writers did not intend for their writings to replace Torah. The writers appear unaware that someday their Aramaic writings about the amazing life and Torah teachings of Yeshua would be used to supercede Torah

Pagan. A noun. Synonyms: gentile, foreigner, *goyim*, sinner. Refers to anyone who is not a descendant of Jacob *or* who does not observe Torah. As an adjective: unrighteous, wicked, adulterous or referring to other non Torah practices of gentiles including religious, civil, historical and linguistic. A pagan is someone who is not following the path of Torah. It simply means No Torah. A person who follows NT practices in conflict with Torah practices is a pagan. This book was written to a presumed audience of pagans unaware of their negative status with Yehovah.

Petroglyphs. For our purposes these are millions of pairs of footprints in family groups which were carved in rocks by the eyewitnesses of Torah as evidence to show that they had traveled there. They took this promise literally:

'Wherever the sole of your foot steps will be yours; your territory will extend from the desert to the L'vanon (Lebanon)) and from the River, the Euphrates River to the Western Sea (Mediterranean). No one will be able to withstand you; Yehovah your God will place the fear and dread of you on all the land you step on, as He told you." Deut. 11, 24+25 CJB

Some day, a prophesied day, the nations dwelling in all of the Middle East will become very aware of the existence of these carvings in their lands: Israel, Syria, Iraq, Iran, Jordan, Saudi Arabia and Egypt. America doesn't have any.

Prayer. In Judaism, Christianity and for the Messianics it is believed to be the basis for maintaining a personal relationship with the Almighty. Here's the sequence of its origins. First, man was created in Yehovah's image, making verbal interaction possible. Second, Adam walked and talked with Yehovah in person on a daily basis. Next, conversing directly with God was validated for all the rest of us human beings when the entire nation of Yisrael heard the Ten Words in the voice of Yehovah. THAT makes it personal. Last, 2 Chronicles and Hosea 14 demonstrate that the people were caught up in situations where many were unable to cleanse themselves to assemble for Passover. Passover that year became an impossibility for the entire nation. The man of God for Israel intervened with Yehovah who listened to him and to his **prayer** of atonement for the people. Yehovah accepted Hezekiah's prayer and cleansed and healed the people without changing Torah.

The oldest prayer in Torah is called the Aaronic Prayer (Numbers 6, 22 to 27). It was given by Moshe on behalf of his older brother Aaron and Aaron's priestly sons. It is used as a way of blessing the children of one's family by calling the Name and Face of 𐤉𐤄𐤅𐤄 upon them.[83] Hebrews interpret it as only applicable to them. It should also be applicable to sojourners with Israel and especially their children. Two silver amulets with this prayer inscribed upon the inside of the roll in Aramaic were found in the 1960s by Dr. Gabriel Barkay, archaeologist with Bar Ilam University. They looked like cigarette butts. The amulet inscriptions are the earliest known of any Scripture or prayer and date before 801 B.C.E. The wearing of this prayer amulet **is** a Torah observance.[84] They are also mini palimpsests. Underneath the inscription a *much older* biblical quotation was found by NASA's high tech means. So much for E hypotheses.

Nehemiah Gordon and Keith Johnson have written an interesting book concerning their personal exploration in Israel of the geographical and linguistic origins of the "Our Father" prayer titled: *A Prayer to Our Father*. Nehemiah. Gordon is a Karaite Jew and expert linguist in ancient Semitic languages. Keith Johnson is a Hebraic roots oriented Christian minister and fluent in Hebrew. Keith Johnson, a Sojourner, is blessed with his own authentic ancient Hebrew Torah scroll! This fact began the lifelong friendship of a Methodist minister and a Karaite Jew: **Yehovah!**

Promised Land. All the land from the Nile River to Lebanon and from the Euphrates River to the western or Mediterranean Sea. All the land whereupon trod the feet of the descendants of Israel while following Yehovah's cloud forty years in the desert wilderness after exiting Egypt. Footprint petroglyphs in the millions are found in

---

[83] *Numbers 6, 22 to 27.*
[84] *Deuteronomy 6, 8 and 9.*

desert areas throughout many middle eastern countries including Palestine, Syria, Iraq, Iran, Saudi Arabia and Jordan. The petroglyphs validate these expanded boundaries of the Promised Land far beyond tiny Israel. This is Big Israel.

Rapture. The Christian church teaches this legend and it is useful in demonstrating their contention that Christians have replaced Israel as the apple of God's Eye. Semitic Scripture never says that Yehovah has any plans to live with His people anywhere other than on His land, eretz Israel.[85] Everything centers on the land of Israel. North America is not mentioned. Heaven anywhere other than earth is not mentioned for future human life. The Promised Land is not in America. America has no petroglyphs of footprints left by the nation of Israel. Secondly, the "Second Coming" Scriptural references point to the return of Yehovah Himself who came here to earth apparently *many* years before the Torah giving at Mt. Sinai *circa* 1500 B.C.E. Hundreds of years later, before 605 B.C.E., His Presence was observed leaving the Jerusalem Temple and the Temple Mount some period of time before Judah was taken into captivity in 605. Unlike all other religions whose objective is a good life in a spiritual world beyond earth, the Hebrew Scriptures repeatedly speak of Yehovah as living in the land of Israel with all thirteen tribes of the nation, and His gentiles, all of his people, in a new society governed by Torah. *Heaven* therefore is on earth.

Here's the Scriptural sequence: First, a succession of long dormant prophecies will come to fruition, starting with the world's oldest occupied city, Damascus Syria becoming a smoking black hole in the ground,. It could start this year or nine hundred years from now. Then, members of the ten tribes of the lost house of Israel and later gentiles will receive Torah teachings from twelve thousand teachers from each of the twelve nonAaronic tribes in a world wide revival consisting of total return to Torah. THEN, there will be no need for teaching about Yehovah, because all will have Torah inscribed in our hearts, Jeremiah 31, 31 to 33. Following this, the events of the *Great Day* will unfold. We will go from a world of 10,000 religions to a Torah observant world ready for the return of the Creator to His Sanctuary.

Salvation. 1. Deliverance of God's Chosen Witnesses from conquerors such as Egypt whose captivity interfered with their Torah lifestyle and worship of Yehovah; 2. Yehovah's *Sojourner* provision for gentiles to obtain the blessings of God by uniting with His witnesses in Torah observance; 3. Yehovah's direct expressed promise to the Rechabite clan of Canaanites that He would ensure there will "never cease to be a Rechabite man *standing before Me*", Jeremiah ch. 35!! This wonderful act of Yehovah

---

[85] *Deuteronomy 11, 12.*

demonstrates for us **fulfillment** of the fifth commandment to *honor your father and mother that your days upon this earth will be long.* Exodus 20,12. This is a Torah Pearl. Read Jeremiah ch 35 or you will miss it. **Yehovah!**

Scriptures v. scriptures. With capital S: The Torah (Genesis through Deuteronomy) specifically and also Torah used in the larger sense, the complete Tanakh or " Old Testament". With a small s: All other old Semitic writings from the Holy Land not written in the Tanakh ("Old Testament").

Second Coming. In the Scriptures this refers to an act of Yehovah, not Jesus. The central event dominating all the writings of the prophets is the Great Day when Yehovah Himself makes His return to earth, His Second Coming. Ironically, Scriptures documenting this are the same Scriptures that Yeshua quoted. Yehovah was in the land of Canaan before the Israelites arrived. He wrote His Name on the mountains near Beit El. His Presence was observed at Mt. Sinai when He gave Israel the Ten Words (the Ten Commandments) and gave Moshe more Instructions over the 40 years of following The Almighty's cloud through the desert. His Presence went with Israel in the Ark of the Covenant. While they were traveling, Yehovah continued giving Torah instructions face to face to Moshe. After forty years of this, Yehovah resided in His Jerusalem Sanctuary, the Holy of Holies in Solomon's Temple on the Temple Mount. Shortly before the second captivity and razing of the first temple in 586 B.C.E., Scripture reports that Yehovah' Presence left the Temple Mount, went out the East Gate, up the Mount of Olives and disappeared into the sky. Therefore, Yehovah's return will be His Second Coming.

Semitic. Refers to three families of more than a dozen languages descended from Shem, one of Noah's three sons. Shem is the root word of *Semites* who are the speakers of these three languages. The two Semitic languages of interest to us are Hebrew and Aramaic.

Servant. Generally refers to the nation of Israel as a whole or to the faithful within the nation. Leviticus 25, 55: **"For the children of Israel are servants to me".** Bankrupt pagans should not denigrate people identified by Yehovah as His servants.

Shema or Sh'ma. Pronounced she MAH. This is the original statement of faith, recited by observant Jews including Jesus three times a day. It proclaims Yehovah as One God. Yeshua recited it as part of his daily observance of Torah. He was a monotheist. Yeshua declared it to be the most important commandment as well as the core of true religion. Many observant Jews have repeated " God is One" as their dying words. It can be found in Deuteronomy 6, 4 and 5. This Shema was repeated to Israel by Moshe in his last sermon to them. See footnote 50.

"Sh'ma Y'ISRAEL! Adonai ELOHEINU, Adonai echad. [Hear, Israel! Adonai our God, Adonai is one]; and you are to love Adonai your God with all your heart, all your being and all your resources." Complete Jewish Bible.

Churches do not teach Sh'ma. Church teachings do not duplicate the lifelong personal conduct of their master Jesus. As repeated three times daily by Yeshua in his own prayer life, the Shema is not a new commandment but a REMINDER that Yehovah is One. Further, Yeshua said [*Think not that I have come to change the Torah. I have not come to change it but to fulfill it. I tell you that not the tiniest stroke of the pen in the written Torah will be changed as long as there is earth and sky and one descendant of Israel in existence.*] Theology has bankrupted everything.

Sojourner. Sojourners biblically were originally Torah keeping gentiles who left Egypt with Israel, traveled with the nation of Israel *and* united with worship of their One and Only Living God, unlike the "mixed multitude". Americans and Christians should rejoice in this original thinking of the Almighty. It is His Provision for including foreigners into the blessings promised to the nation of Yisrael. The rationales provided by religions that say you need another savior or even a co-savior are a major **revocation** to the Almighty's Words. In other words gentiles should be adjusting to the reality of Yehovah's Words in Torah, such as in Isaiah 43,11. *I, even I, am that I am, And besides Me there is no savior.* Hebrews and sojourners have no Scriptural requirement to adjust to the man made teachings of any church, nor be judged by any pagan. Since the tribes of Israel are scattered all over the globe, there is hope for Torah observing gentiles who have not moved to the land of Israel. Anyone lives the life of a Torah observant sojourner retains all the rights of one who is born in the land. This is so that there will be only one Torah for all. The Church nullifies "one Torah for all", by replacing Torah with new Salvation provisions for gentiles whom their theology then indicts as guilty using the concept *Law* as a perversion of Torah. Foreign university students who come to America to study and appear in church are called sojourners. If you go with the teachings of men in all this, you are telling the Almighty Creator of the Universe that you don't like His ideas about how you should live your life. You are telling Him that you intend to continue not taking His Path *a la* Jeremiah 6,16. Nice going. Poke your finger in the Almighty's eye.

Stoning. The capital punishment for breaking Torah. For example the people must stone to death anyone who is *found* to not be observing the Sabbath. BUT, death provisions of Torah are presently very rarely carried out in Israel. The current situation is that many of the descendants of Yisrael live in exile under jurisdictions of foreign governments. And, the people living in the land of Israel are not living under the authority of Yehovah's Torah such as we did when Yehovah's Presence actually dwelt in the land of Israel from infinity to *circa* 900 B.C.E. Considering how all the prophets died, including Yeshua, Israel is reluctant to carry out Yehovah's life taking judgements in the absence of His Presence presiding over His Torah government.

Tanakh. Ta Na Kh. An acronym for the Hebrew words: *T*orah, *N*evi'im, and *K*'tuvim, corresponding to Torah, Prophets and Writings. Religions call the Tanakh by the detestable term "Old Testament" which is a pagan anti Semitic term avoided by this book. Jesus promoted Tanakh to be **equal** to the words of Yehovah. Jesus said:

"The Tanakh says, 'Man does not live on bread alone, but on every word that comes from the mouth of Adonai'" Matthew 4,4.

Torah. Torah means teaching of Yehovah's ancient Ways. By convention, *Torah proper* refers to the five scrolls or written Torah of Moshe, the oldest, most sacred part of Tanakh (*Torat Moshe*)[86]. *Generically* Torah is used to refer to the entire OT, the Tanakh. Since an illiterate gentile cannot tell what is valid commentary on Torah, other sacred books in Judaism, such as the Talmud, Mishna, Gemara are outside the scope of this book, as is Judaism. Torah is life instructions to the people of Israel given to Moshe by the Almighty at Mount Sinai and throughout many lands of the Middle East some 3500 years ago. The entire nation heard the first Ten Words for themselves in the voice of the Almighty which were later written on stone tablets by the finger of God in Paleo Hebrew. Then Moses heard Yehovah's additions to the Ten Words in face to face conversations with Him. Moshe received these additional instructions (torahs) from Yehovah during the 40 years as the entire nation followed Yehovah's cloud throughout the middle east, headed for the Promised Land, Canaan. These additional torahs along with the writing of the circumstances of its history, resulted in five scrolls of Torah. Torah is known in the western world as Genesis, Exodus, Leviticus, Numbers and Deuteronomy. Torah documents torahs given by Yehovah to the nation as well as to His messenger Moses. The number of torahs is far larger than Maimonides *circa*. 1100s C.E. who tabulated **613** written torahs in an effort to coordinate Torah of Moshe with the written traditions of the ancient rabbis. Torah of Moshe contains thousands of torahs, depending upon various categories dreamed up.[87]

Tradition. A pattern of behavior, or actions, based upon a group ethic or value system which is inherited by default and originates from an earlier or higher source. In this book traditional Christian teachings are presented as the default inheritance of the western world, for which Torah is the earlier and higher source. Yehovah does not like

---

[86] *[And Moses wrote the Torah.] Deuteronomy 31, 9 to 12.*
[87] *See the comprehensive "The Complete Concordance of Torah Commandments" by David D. Mahoney.*

being worshiped by the commandments (traditions) of men, only by His Torah traditions. Read Isaiah 29, 13 to 16 in a Hebraic translation, true to the Hebrew.

Ur of the Chaldees. An ancient city in southern Iraq which is still inhabited to this day. Abraham was a native of Ur. The USA liberated it in the 1990s C.E. from the dictator Saddam Hussein. Ur is the city Daniel was taken to during the nation of Israel's captivity in Babylon. He was enslaved and taken from the land of Israel to Babylonia. After a decade in prison, Daniel became the second wealthiest person in all of Babylonia by interpreting dreams of Babylonian royalty. Daniel was a eunuch. He had no children. What became of his wealth? It was put in trust to operate the library or institution of higher learning in Ur! The library consisted of the learned or wise men from Israel who were astronomers. Daniel received advance knowledge of future events in Yehovah's Plan for earth. Some call these Messianic events. The point is, Yehovah revealed to Daniel the astrological signs of changes in the constellations[88] that would signal each new development in the earth's future prophetic events. Daniel revealed *some* of this knowledge to his group of astrological astronomers. He funded their search of the heavens forever (a very long time) so that someone here on earth would be watching the heavens for the secret signs signaling the fulfillment of prophetic events in God's plan for earth. Five hundred years later, according to the NT account, when wise men saw the signs of an anointed one and followed The Star, they came with expensive gifts of gold, frankincense and myrrh, using Daniel's stored wealth *and* secret astrological knowledge. That is the story and Scripture is clear that not all of God's revelations to Daniel were passed on to his astronomers. In other words, all facts point to Jesus as a messiah, an anointed one, not yet **the** Messiah. It points to the arrival of Yeshua as Torah and Prophecy in the flesh. The story is ongoing. To this day we do not know the rest of the prophetic knowledge revealed to Daniel by Yehovah. Daniel was ordered not to reveal all details. There are more astrological events to come. Presently only about half of biblical prophecy has been fulfilled.

Yahu. An abbreviated form of the Name of Yehovah. It consists of the first three of the four letters yod hei vav hei. (The vav was in later times given the sound of a U). This term also refers to the Anointed Ones or prophets of Israel. All the names of the prophets end in *yahu*: Yeshiyahu is Isaiah; Yermiyahu is Jeremiah. These

---

[88] *Astrology, as used by human beings developed after people noticed the relationship between constellation events and earthly events. The human practice of astrology is condemned in Scripture, human beings use astrology for their own purposes (money, power). It is the practice of pagans. Astrology is Yahweh's. The constellations are set up by the Almighty as timepiece hands announcing to earth the arrival of prophetic events on His Clock. Adam named earth's animals. Yahweh named the constellations.*

examples speak to the depth of meaning inherent in the individual sounds of the Aleph Beit, wherein the names of the prophets tell you that they speak as the mouthpiece of Yehovah. The present leader of Israel is Benjamin Netan*yahu*.

Yehovah. Spelled *yod hei vav hei*, it is the Name the Almighty One of Israel calls Himself. It is His personal Name spelled out, meaning "I will be that I will be". ☛ *"This is how you will refer to Me for all time."* Variously pronounced as Yehovah, Yahweh, Yihweh, or Yahoveh. Yehovah was written as 𐤉𐤄𐤅𐤄 and later as יהוה the same letters (reversed order), but shaped differently. Jewish persons do not write or say the Name Yehovah choosing instead the term *Adonai* or simply or *HaShem* meaning "the Name". So in the very first verse of their bible it is written, *In the beginning the name created the heavens and the earth"*. They are the descendants of those who created the Scriptures; This is a very complex issue; Foreigners do not understand it; Therefore gentiles should not condemn. As Hebrews read the written word Yehovah, they respectfully say aloud "Adonai". It is a beautiful word. Unlike all other names throughout the entire history human life here on planet earth, it is only true that when the Name of Yehovah is spoken or written, it simultaneously invokes the Presence of Yehovah! Reproducing His Name does not go UNNOTICED. Are you ready to suddenly have the Presence of Yehovah join you in a situation where you used His Name without thinking? Probably not. See the problem? If you even KNOW the Name, you are ahead of most people who have ever lived on earth. All the saints of the Almighty who lived before Moshe did not know the Name. But you know it and you could begin calling on the Name of Yehovah now.

Yeshua. Also **Y'shua**. Literally *Yah + Shua* meaning yod hei vav hei + redeemer. In the western gentile world Yehovah is not the ONLY savior. But, see Isaiah 43, 10 to 13. The word *Jesus* has NO intrinsic meaning.

Yeshua ben Yosef ha Maschiach. Literally in English: Yeshua, son of Joseph, the Messiah. This is the name for Jesus of Nazareth according to gentiles who are Messianic believers.

Yeshuaites. A term of convenience grabbed by this author for this book. The first generation aboriginal followers of Yeshua. After Yeshua's passing they operated out of Jerusalem a "love of Torah" ministry for the house of Israel. They reproduced Jesus' teachings as they had witnessed them. Led by James the *Just*, the brother of Jesus, they reproduced Yeshua's lifestyle, teachings and doctrine as they witnessed. Details of these Torah teachings and doctrines are minimized in the NT, but alluded to in other historical sources of the period. *Just* means Torah keeper.

Chapter 11

Yehovah's Torah Way of Life

Torah provides us with a lifestyle centered upon His ancient Ways. On an objective basis, a perspective of Hebrew scriptures is useful to us only if it *connects* the words and events in all the Hebrew's heritage writings in continuity.[89] Semitic perspectives such as the one used here are the only approaches which complete the puzzle of information from all the ancient Semitic writings about Yehovah. This is true of Scriptures such as Tanakh and also NT scriptures and other historic Hebrew writings, including historical first century writings such as those of Josephus. The Hebraic perspective of this book enables the connection of Tanakh and NT into **one continuous Torah story**. Yehovah's Ways do not change, nor should their story. Yehovah's Torah Ways are the nexus for Tanakh and the information from NT writings and antiquities finds. Now if NT or Josephus's writings have factual errors, that is no blemish on a Semitic perspective of Torah because the framework this perspective creates acts to *highlight* factual errors. Identifying errors improves fidelity to His Ways. This is true of the NT's errors[90] in spite of NT western traditions which say the NT is the *improved word of God,* better and more sacred than Torah which it replaces. **A magic outcome**, totally dependent upon *faith* [91]. Actually, Torah provides the concrete foundation with which to view all the Torah teachings found in the NT section of the western bible. Any NT events and teachings not in Torah are fabricated for religion's sake. Both Hebrew Tanakh and Aramaic NT illustrate that Yeshua's subsequent teachings in NT events are Torah commentary. They are also commentary

---

[89] *Any other choice produces the free for all of 34,800+ ☥ religions.*
[90] *The NT has an arithmetic error in group 3 of its **very first** claim (Matt.1 to 17).*
[91] *Jeremiah 6, 19 and 20.*

on themes close to Yehovah's heart, His Ways, noted in Torah and meant to herd us back to the Almighty. Any themes in any version of the NT or in other writings that do not *spring* from Torah identify that writing as destructive change to Torah. That is true of the Latinized Greek Torah and NT *books* that in the 1600s were translated into King James English; The KJV is the theological springboard for English bibles.

The belief that the modern NT characterizes Jesus' life and teachings as replacing Torah violates a direct command from Yehovah.[92] The characters identified in NT period events were 99.9% Jewish people who knew Torah as their bible. Jesus' bible was Torah. Torah authentically documents Yehovah intervening in and identifying with Jewish history, language and culture. Torah is the written documentation of 𐤉𐤄𐤅𐤄 personally experienced by the nation of Israel. The preceding chapters in this book detailed these Jewish scenarios interacted by Yehovah.

If you are not Jewish, the option afforded by Torah to obtain the blessings of the Almighty is to follow Torah as a sojourner with Israel. You cannot become a sojourner with Israel without personally adopting some legitimate Semitic perspective of Torah, or you will not have Torah honestly in your heart. This book describes a composite but bona fide Hebraic perspective of Torah found in available English language sources during the author's research timeline. Composite refers to its genesis in Hebrew experts from different areas of expertise including their individual sub categories: ancient language, archaeology, geography, history. All are linked by their Semitic perspective of ancient biblical phenomena. There are obviously other Semitic perspectives which differ from the ones described here. Who is to judge for or against them? Not me. Using the present approach, every gentile has the wherewithal to unite with Israel by observing the teachings of Torah in daily, weekly, monthly and yearly personal behavior. See # 3 below. Torah teachings which apply to everyone can *mostly* be easily understood and deliberately practiced. If we know Torah well enough to know Yehovah's Ways, Torah's teachings are not too hard for us. We are not doomed to failure and hopelessly in need of mercy from any savior other than Yehovah. There is Torah precedence for mercy when the nation of Israel was traveling and unable to accomplish certain acts required for participation in Passover. The chief priest, Hezekiah, one year obtained forgiveness for the entire nation of Israel by pleading directly with Yehovah. Yehovah's mercy left Torah unchanged; 2) There was mercy for gentiles attempting to keep Torah by trusting God while traveling with Israel away

---

[92]*Jeremiah 6, 19 and 20. In vain people worship me, preferring their own manmade rules to My Torah. I will bring disaster upon them.*

from Egypt. Those gentiles became Yehovah's "My Gentiles" through the fact of their Torah observance. Their precedent proofs the gentile pathway to Yehovah's blessings; 3) Torah is portrayed as *one Torah for all*. Gentile sojourners receive this standing, their acceptance by Yehovah, as they receive "all the rights of one born in the land" of Israel. This standing is objective proof of the **operational definition of redemption. One is personally united with the nation of Israel.** Torah requirements are far more achievable than what church teachings have represented to gentiles as their proof of salvation. Can men confer the Almighty's blessings? Which of the 43,800 church traditions define the process? Do church traditions motivate Yehovah? Do we want to conduct our lives in harmony with the words of men or with the Words of the Creator of the universe? Are we pleasing men or the Creator? **Before Yehovah, we are responsible for a lot less than we are when we allow ourselves to be judged by church traditions.** Torah is not theoretical, it's down to earth. It's not thinking, its habits. There are Uncertain issues of Torah and they are up to the individual to apply as long as one does not change Torah and continues the observant life (mainly: Eat the Passover meal). Torah is security; It is not too hard, not beyond our reach. In keeping Torah "do not allow any pagan to judge you" (a favorite saying of Michael Rood).

At this point in the book, you the reader have been introduced to descriptions of God's Ways contrasted with the teachings of western religions. The religious *struggle* for gentiles, evangelizing, is an issue highlighted by Shaul throwing James the Just down the temple steps; It is still with us. Yehovah's Ways reside today in the original meanings of Scripture from a virtual storehouse of Hebraic perspectives available nowadays in English. From this introduction offered by GHR, I hope you will embrace other sources to understand and know Yehovah and to establish your Hebraic perspective. On this journey, I hope you will enjoy a newfound sense of personal freedom. As I am only a short distance further down the path in front of you, my fellow foreigners, I am extremely hesitant to give specific advice. We all need help. While all the earth awaits the return of Yehovah, you could settle on reading Torah and Tanakh using ***Tanakh: the Holy Scriptures***, particularly the Jewish Publication Society's ***Jewish Study Bible***. The ***Complete Jewish Bible*** is always helpful, starting with the detailed *Introduction*. To help you point yourself toward many unfamiliar Torah observances and to free yourself from looping back into the dead end trail of religious thinking, I'll go *way out on a limb* and say here are 7 observations, things I have thought about trying, tried, am trying or have tried to try:

1. Hebrew. An achievable approach for many is learn to read Torah in modern Hebrew symbols. One can more easily learn the original pictographic Hebraic aleph beit with their concrete meanings to have some idea what Words God revealed to the

ancients. But, avoid spiritualized descriptions of pictographs which read modern foreign theology into their meanings. Every week listen for part of Shabbat to Nehemiah Gordon explain the lost significance of ancient Hebrew words and the wonderful pearls of Torah in the Torah Pearls section at www.truth2u.org.

2. Torah. Change out your old pagan mental structures with your new knowledge of Torah. Find for yourself Rabbi Mordecai Alfandari's list of torahs. They apply to everyone and provide a way for Yehovah's people to identify the Way of Torah each of us is meant to observe. Educate yourself with Nehemiah Gordon's newsletter teachings from www.KaraiteKorner.org. Read the Jewish Publication Societies' *The Jewish Study Bible*'s Tanakh translation. ☞ Listen to Nehemiah Gordon, Keith Johnson and Jono Vandor's Torah Pearls "through the bible" weekly radio broadcast at truth2u.org. Past broadcasts are recorded and freely available 24/7 at the web site, starting with Genesis 1. This is essential, the most important and efficient way to start learning the ancient meanings of Torah and the ancient customs of the Hebrews. I know this from personal experience mostly too late for this book's research. And there is the awe of listening to a sojourner Methodist minister juggle his church traditions with Hebraic perspective going through the Torah with Jono Vandor and Nehemiah Gordon. Work on getting rid of all your western gentile pagan ways and religious practices. Study David Mahoney's The Complete Concordance of Torah Commandments. It organizes torahs around several views of Torah's instructions, one view is torahs that apply to everyone. Caveat, many of Torah's provisions cannot be carried out because the house of Israel is dispersed throughout the world, the Presence of Yehovah is not on the land of Israel and there is no temple, nor organized priesthood of genetic descendants of Aaron. This is why Reformed Judaism exists. With this perspective in mind do not, for example, advocate death for someone who fails to keep the Sabbath. Do not fret over Torah instructions which have become *impossible* to observe in foreign lands: Eat The Meal on Passover.

3. Teacher. Find a Hebrew who observes the written Torah of Moshe willing to teach Torah truths. Read all of Nehemiah Gordon's writings, starting with *The Hebrew Yeshua V. The Greek Jesus*. Get on the email list of the KaraiteKorner website for Nehemiah's newsletter. Become very familiar with that website. Become a Karaite sourced sojourner. Think like a Karaite. Nehemiah's teachings are carefully worded in respect to Torah and very complete. In my house, we listen to him weekly on **Truth2You** radio broadcasts on the internet. Need a hero? Find out what Nehemiah Gordon has to say about Rabbi Mordecai Alfandari. The Torah minded experts identified in the acknowledgments section of this book are true modern day heroes.

4. Calendar Observances. Celebrate the appointed feasts of Adonai at the appointed times as found in Leviticus 23, observing these appointed times using His lunar calendar which starts each year when the barley crop is *aviv* in *eretz Israel*. See lunar calendar information on Karaite website. Observe Sabbath on the correct day. Recite the Sh'ma daily. Reject Easter and Christmas as pagan religious holidays. Reaffirm your heart as a sojourner by observing the Passover Sacrifice (EAT THE MEAL) on the day determined by the new moon barley aviv reports from Jerusalem.

5. Report only to Yehovah. Follow His Words only. Discard gentile tithing schemes on income derived from foreign lands. Tithes only apply to income from *eretz Israel*. Implement Psalm 1, 2 in your family. Marry a sojourner. We need more of 'em. Become one. Teach this Torah to your children and read it to them. Pray that they will love to explore Torah and celebrate His Feasts. Recite over them the Aaronic prayer (Numbers 6, 22 to 27); Read to them Psalm 1 and Psalm 91. For a time, read Proverbs 31, 10 to 31 to your wife (read Psalm 112 to your husband) every Sabbath as they describe the ideals of both roles. Note the *differences* with the roles in western society. Recite the Aaronic prayer over your spouse when you leave each other.

6. Provide Mercy. If you absolutely have to have routine religious experiences, spend more time reading Torah and act to do justice and provide mercy for widows, orphans and those truly crying out for mercy. Pray for peace in Israel, grieve over pagan practices which continue on Yehovah's land. *Support* the nation of Israel.

7. Unity. For those of us who have not had the Hebrews' familial experiences with Yehovah and who live in a pagan land half way around the earth, implementing Yehovah's instructions in Torah will require phase in time. For western gentiles, observing His Holy Feasts will occur in apparent isolation from most all the other Torah observant peoples worldwide. In the last decade researching and writing this book, I have not met another gentile in person who practices Torah observance solely from the elements of a Jewish Torah perspective. However observing Yehovah's words **no matter what** is the sojourner mission. And, it remains true that all of the torah steps mentioned throughout this book is kid's stuff for an observant Jew. Know that you will be united with His people around the world, all of us showing up when He shows up; Gathering together with Yehovah, at His appointed times and customs; Synchronized by the unity of His lunar calendar's timetable. Understand the unity prayer of Jesus with this observing of Torah's feasts in worldwide unity with His People in mind. In this way we gentiles to live out Torah and Jesus' teachings in perfect unity.

I hope these 7 observations will be a blessing for you.

Chapter 12

Co Stars of the NT

After finishing the initial draft of this book, two big issues persisted in my mind unaddressed so far in the book.[93] The first issue involved missing information on key figures in the book we could refer to as *Some of the* ACTS *of the Jewish Fans of Yeshua*. To complete this book I also needed to deal with a large amount of information demonstrating the prolific substitution of a new development, the "Gospel", in exchange for Jesus' teachings of Torah. In that regard, it came to me that I had gathered enough information from several Hebraic sources to describe a historical vacuum labeled here the First Generation Void. It is the time period between the death of Yeshua, call it 30 C.E., and the death of Jerusalem's Judaic society in 70 C.E. when Rome completed the destruction of Jerusalem. Some refer to this as the Judeo Christian period, but, as of the passing of Yeshua, the apostles had not yet been called Christians. Also the term is used by modern Christians to refer to a period of time in which many Torah and Judeo elements have been *excised* from the written NT in favor of faith teachings. From only the NT account, we know little of what the first generation followers of Yeshua's did after his passing. The record of their doctrinal life is omitted. Hence the word Void. In GHR these first generation followers of Jesus are called *Yeshuaites*. Whatever one calls them, they are important because they complete the NT's story in its first five books so that we know how the original followers of Yeshua implemented his teachings during that first forty years following his passing. Could we understand the American Revolution if we omit the first forty years of American history after the Revolutionary War victory and omit the existence of the

---

[93] *These may be difficult to swallow, but we should all know what Hebrews report as the facts of their own history in their experience.*

Declaration of Independence? Hebrew historical sources show Yeshua teaching Torah. A reading of the Christian NT using Hebrew perspectives of various words reveals that also. The word Christian is not a creation of the first generation Yeshuaites. It is a foreign term which the apostles were called later, in Antioch, Turkey which was pagan gentile country and the early stomping grounds of Paul. If we consider other historical, archaeological and linguistic evidence of the time period from our Hebrew perspective, then we can fill in biblically relevant information about the Yeshuaites' Torah doctrines. We have to do it that way because somehow the history of the Yeshuaites was left out of the Acts account of the Jewish apostles. Either that or any writings of the apostles at the Jerusalem headquarters were for some reason later deleted from Acts, possibly in subsequent *translations*. Here's what is known.

Who were the leaders of the Yeshuaites? James (the brother of Yeshua) and also Peter. However, everyone, even Peter reported to James!!!!!!

Who were the competitors? The Pharisees led by Shaul and the Sadducees who were liaisoned with the local government of the Roman authorities. Rome considered Yeshuaites to be political rebels, terrorists. Hence, *believers* v. lions.

How did the Yeshuaites operate in their Jerusalem headquarters? James and Peter carried on the Torah teachings of Yeshua. The headquarters building was a large stone structure in Jerusalem. It's huge foundation stones have been identified in Jerusalem. The building contained sleeping quarters, kitchen and even its own synagogue. It housed the "upper room" so prominent in the story of the *Ruach ha Kodesh* (Holy Spirit) found in Acts. Over this forty years, while Israel dispersed throughout other lands, the Yeshuaite operation spread throughout all big Israel, the 300,000 square miles. Aside from writings such as those of the Essenes found in the Dead Sea scrolls, there is little direct information. It seems obvious that if they had their own synagogue, then they had their own copies of the Torah scrolls as well as their own priests who implemented Torah observances duplicating the teachings of Yeshua. The Yeshuaites had at least one powerful friend on the Sanhedrin. The NT points out that a man named Joseph of Arimathea had enough influence to obtain the body of Yeshua from Pilate for burial. He is biblically presented as a counselor representing the Judean city of Ramtha. He was thus a member of the ruling body of Judaism, the Sanhedrin. He is identified in the NT as a good and righteous man. Those two words in our Hebraic perspective mean that he loved and observed written Torah of Moshe. The point of all this is that the Yeshuaites had a powerful friend in the Sanhedrin who shared their doctrine of Torah observance. In the history of Israel there has always been a "remnant" of people who remained faithful to the written Torah of Moshe. They exist today. In this case it was Joseph and the Yeshuaites. Yet where are Yeshuaite Torah teachings and activities presented in the book of Acts? Nowhere; *Gospel* or *Good News* is substituted. The teachings of Yeshua centered around returning all the people to observance of the written Torah of Moshe. Yeshua was constantly exposing the conflicts created by the ancient rabbanites's changes to Mosaic Torah. This motivation existed in every encounter Yeshua had with rabbis and leaders of sects of Judaism.

As the power of the Pharisees over Judaism declined, the Sadduccees became the dominant sect. They pointed out to Roman authorities that since they were dominant over the Pharisees they should be allowed to *operate* Judaism throughout the land of Judea. A huge power grab. Rome agreed to this arrangement because it was not interested in getting bogged down in local religious squabbles. All Rome wanted was to collect the tribute *money* from the province with as few problems as possible. By 68 C.E. it became apparent that the Sadducees had failed and the province was out of control. So the Roman army destroyed Jerusalem by 70 C. E., and paraded 4,000 slaves, the solid gold Menorah, Temple accessories and Temple treasure (bank reserve) of gold ingots (talents) throughout the streets of Rome. They scattered the inhabitants throughout the empire and used the Temple gold to pay for building the Coliseum in Rome. There is nothing left of the Yeshuaite Jerusalem headquarters building but the foundation stones. James and Peter's Yeshuaite operation evaporated. Everyone was instantly a war refugee with no country. A huge vacuum developed as a result of the loss of control of Judaism. Shaul found his services no longer needed in the land of Israel as a Roman government informant. Reinventing himself, Shaul stepped in to seize what was left of the Yeshuaite operation existing in gentile country to the North (where he grew up) as his base of operation. The first goal: somehow, become a Christian. Hence, a self described miracle conversion on the road to Damascus.

Shaul

Shaul, pronounced Shaw OOL, was born in Turkey. He was accustomed to being around gentiles, casting some doubt upon his observance of Torah as a rabbi! An educated man and knowledgeable of foreign cultures, he was undoubtedly exposed to the teachings of classical Greek thinkers. From historical accounts, he was prominent in one of the sects of Judaism. And, his troubles with the Roman government were quite minimal. According to the reports of both Josephus and the early church father *Clement*, Shaul's brief prison stays were minimum security and appear to have been "staged" in order to protect his status with the local Roman government as an informant on the Yeshuaites. The Roman government eventually considered the Jewish community led by James the Just, the brother of Jesus to be rebels and terrorists. In time, Shaul's persecution of Yeshuaites ceased as his status as a government informant diminished. That's the setting.

In 2 Corinthians 11 in general and verse 4 in particular it says *false apostles will teach another Jesus, another spirit and another gospel which you have not received from us.* Shaul was lamenting his competition, the other pseudo emissaries of Yeshua, who apparently were also duplicating Shaul's methods to establish their own new churches. Do not be deceived by the phrase, *"which you have not received from us"*. Shaul did not bring the same message from Jerusalem that Yeshua, Peter and James taught. He is talking about His version of Yeshua's teachings, the gospel. He is not referring to the Torah teachings given to the original apostles by Yeshua, nor other "gospels." Ironically verse 4 is also prophetic of the Roman Emperor Constantine's destruction of all things Hebrew in the 4th century C.E. In Galatians 1, 6 and 7 it says that some have already embraced another Gospel which is not even another gospel but rather a perversion of the gospel of Messiah. This is truly reprehensible on Shaul's part. Shaul's "gospel" IS a perversion of Yeshua's Torah centered life and teaching. The Galatians of the first century were already boldly modifying the Hebrew Gospels of Matthew, Mark, Luke and John to deJudaize teaching the Gospel accounts for better palatability among THEIR gentiles. Enquiring minds might wonder just how many versions of Yeshua's life and gospels *were* circulating in the first century?

In the Jerusalem Temple there was a special section for gentiles who loved the God of Israel and the Hebrew Torah. They are referred to in English bibles by the term God Fearers, which we prefer to call by the Torah term sojourners. Shaul sat with them Now why would he do that? Was he considered a gentile? No, he was a well known rabbi. Was he there to "work" the gentiles? Historical documents report a physical altercation occurred on the temple steps in which Shaul threw James the Just down the steps! Shaul, right on the Temple Mount, was proselytizing these God fearing, Torah keeping, sojourner gentiles with a new religious agenda eventually labeled *the Gospel*. Was James in his way? James continued to reproduce his brother's teachings which could be described as "Return to Yehovah's Torah". The "Gospel" Shaul touted in various epistles in the NT replaced Yeshua's teachings. (Shaul did not personally experience Yeshua's teachings as one of Yeshua's followers). Shaul's Gospel teachings differ from the four original Aramaic and Hebrew "Gospel" *letters* which appear at the beginning of the NT. In Shaul's Gospel, upon which he expounded in his one third of the NT writings, he expounded upon a new set of religious teachings[94] for gentile

---

[94] *Acts 15, verses 19 and 20.*

"believers" to practice. In effect Shaul's gospel teachings resulted in Torah details being diminished throughout the NT. Over time, gentile *believers* outnumbered Hebrews in the synagogue congregations. Gradually, Torah practices were superceded by Shaul's new teachings for gentiles. The Judeo details were omitted from the written NT accounts. Torah was cast off. The apostles became Christians and the new religion labeled Christianity.[95]

From the Hebrew perspective Shaul did not carry on any teachings of his "master" Rabbi Yeshua and Shaul's teachings cannot be called **Judeo** anything. A defining characteristic of this new religion was its emphasis on proselytizing gentiles worldwide. Recall that this is the opposite of what Yeshua and his first generation Yeshuaites lived and taught. How did the treasure of information on Yeshua's Torah teachings to the aboriginal Judeo believers, the *Yeshuaites* get left out of or deleted from Acts? Why were James' activities left out of Acts? Even James' death is omitted from Acts. In Foxe's Book of Martyrs, used by Shakespeare for its many historical details, James is labeled as James **the Less**. It lists him as the brother of Jesus, writer of the epistle and leader of the Jerusalem church after Jesus' passing. One prominent Hebrew Professor and archeologist believes James to be James the Righteous referred to by the writers of the Essenes scrolls. Incredibly, Foxe places this James below the status of James son of Zebedee, the apostle and brother of John!? Not only did Shaul push this James the Just down the steps, *someone* changed James' place in history by excluding his work from Acts. In later translations, before and continuing after Constantine's time, the deJudaizing of the four Gospels was *completed*.[96]

Shaul's conversion experience is suspect. At the time he was traveling with a group of pro Roman government rabbis who would have likely had him immediately stoned to death if they witnessed him becoming a convert to Yeshua's anti Rome and anti rabbinic rebels. Shaul had previously gained his prominence over the years in Pharaseeism through his persecution of Yeshua and his followers. That prominence had been all lost in the year 70 C.E. when Shaul also become an exile. To recover his lost status as a religious leader, Shaul sought to gain control over the now refugee Yeshuaite operation by traveling to the Yeshuaite satellite synagogues (soon to be called churches)

---

[95] *Acts 11,26. Antioch is in Syria.*
[96] *John 5,1 ...***there was a feast of the Jews***...Surely, John knew which feast it was. He also knew it was a feast* **of Yahweh***, only Gentiles ignorant of Torah called it* **of the Jews***.. This is evidence someone changed NT words.*

throughout several foreign lands. Step one, become The Christian. So the Conversion Experience recorded in the NT. His writings in the NT simply chronicle his rise to power. Christianity however does not teach the account of Shaul's activities as the power grab it is, instead explaining his changes to Yeshua's teachings as required to "spread the Gospel". In addition to James, here is another *challenge* to Shaul's goals reported in Acts 17, 10 to 13:

[Now the church at Berea was called the most noble of them all because the leaders there tested all new ideas for conformance to written Torah of Moshe.]

Sounds like applause for the Bereans, but not so. They were a tough nut for Shaul to crack. They stubbornly held to Torah and resisted Shaul's new teachings. It could be that the mysterious "thorn" in Paul's side may in fact have been the Bereans, who refused to give up Yehovah's Torah as their standard of truth and accept Paul's good news gospel teachings as the new Torah. Shaul, or *someone* apparently achieved control over Torah based satellite synagogues in foreign lands by implementing the following adjustments: 1) Original NT letters in Hebrew or Aramaic were put aside in favor of written translations into Greek; Luke himself did this on at least one occasion; 2) Synagogue and "church" leadership not fluent in Greek (that would be ALL the kosher Hebrew priests) were put aside in favor of Greek speaking clergy; I call them clergy because we cannot call them priests since in Torah Yehovah ordered that they be chosen on the basis of tribal genetics, descended from Moses' older brother Aaron; 3) Torah practices were put aside and new worship rules were implemented in the "churches" which favored gentile and foreign language mindsets. Torah's explicit instructions for worship were discarded, as gentiles continued to create religious theological doctrines in which they, the gentiles, replaced the Israelites as the recipients of the Almighty's blessings. Belief and worship in modern Christian churches is descended from these deTorahfied theological writings and practices. The Torah provision for gentile sojourning was gone. **One Torah for all** was gone gone gone. As the years rolled by the notion developed and was implemented that Jesus himself had taught this gospel as his good news message from God which replaced Torah. This is how Shaul and other NT leaders acted to expand their new religion. Under Shaul's leadership a new Torah (NT) was consolidated and Yehovah's Torah teachings replaced with the Good News Gospel. Ironically, the word gospel nowadays implies truth in the nth degree. These actions of Paul suggest those of a Prince of this World and are an example of the sort of individual referred to in Deuteronomy 13.

For a hundred Western generations (two thousand years) God has been silent about this Christian highjacking of Yeshua's message for Israel to return to Torah.

Yeshua's first generation followers, the Yeshuaites are nowhere to be found in the NT. In their place are the activities of Shaul which replaced the Yeshuaite history with new foreign terms: "Judeo Christian", gospel, church, pastor and all the abstract Christian theological principles: salvation (versus being always in the presence of Yehovah); Grace (versus a personality characteristic of Yehovah; Faith (See ch.10, versus trust); Believer (versus observant), etc. As previously related, there is nothing Judeo about theological abstractions. This is why observing Torah in everyday life is so beautiful. Observing Torah is down to earth habits, there are no ongoing changes to them, and no 34,000+ variations of doctrines, only one doctrine: **Torat Moshe**. Christians routinely apply this *Judeo Christian* label to their own present day teachings and assume that the current teachings are what Yeshua and then the first generation Christian followers of Jesus believed during the void period. It should be no surprise that the forty year history of the Yeshuaites is missing from the Acts account. Please do not be misled by Greek based NT scriptures that hail Shaul as a hero in spreading the Gospel of Jesus Christ. That is the plausible explanation which diverts attention from the fact that "spreading the Gospel" was really a systematic replacement of the provisions of Torah which Jesus taught. The features of Gospel teachings amount to a counterfeit religion that Shaul helped invent and label true and holy. Shaul did not carry on ANY of the teachings of Yeshua. Should you trust a person who proudly writes that he will go to any length and assume any false identity to spread the teachings of his new religion? If you do not agree with that statement, read I Corinthians 9, 19 to 25, noting also that Shaul calls himself a *savior* ! But there is a Way to follow both Jesus and Torah.

Yes Adonai has apparently turned His Face and been silent. But it will always be true that His Words (Yehovah's) have creative power in the cosmos and will not return to Him void. The clock is ticking and the Christian church will *Some Day* observe first hand Adonai's vow of judgement as revealed in Jeremiah 6, 19b and 20:

[I am going to bring disaster upon this people. It is the consequence of their own actions. For they do not listen to My words. And as for My Torah, they reject it.]

The Semitic perspective of Hebrew and Aramaic Scriptures described throughout this book leads to the troubling conclusion that Shaul was a Torah breaker who taught others to reject Yehovah's teachings. This was an unanticipated research outcome and expressing it was delayed for as late as possible in this book. If one has listened to Yehovah's words and adopted the Semitic perspective for interpreting Torah, then statements in the NT that are departures from Torah stand out clearly. Yeshua was devoted to returning the lost tribes of Israel to Torah. Yet the experience in the Christian church has always been one of love for Shaul's religion, so much that very few recall the Almighty's Words, that His Torah is His only standard for humanity.

Yeshua

This book started as an idea to correct some common western misconceptions found in the bibles commonly used by Christians. Nowadays, after several thousand years, the people of the western world in some numbers are beginning to acquaint themselves with the Semitic roots of their own bibles. We happen to be living while this is happening! After finishing most of this book, a copy of ***Restoring Abrahamic Faith*** by Dr. James D. Tabor arrived in the mail. Nehemiah Gordon wrote highly of James Tabor's book, so the trail to the Semitic perspective of the Hebrew Scriptures led to him. After a partial read, I reluctantly set it aside while I finished this project. It was too good. There is a beautiful thing Dr. Tabor's book did for me and here it is: I didn't realize that **it is not written** that Yeshua said that he is the Messiah. And **it is not written** that Yeshua said he was God. See for example Matthew 24, 23 to 26. Yeshua as God and Messiah statements are always reported in the NT as being made by other people! It is only written that other people characterized him in those two ways. Even with a reasonable knowledge of scriptures, we err because we do not understand the significance of facts too conveniently overlooked. James Tabor has stepped up and pointed out these *other people* instances which were obvious to him but not to us. Sadly we continue to live oblivious to the real message contained in Scriptures. Man made traditions are effective at misleading us with subtle changes over time.

Yeshua routinely referred to himself as "son of man". Yehovah called Ezekial by this *son of man* title.[97] On the basis of his own words recorded in scriptures, Yeshua thought of himself as the latest in a long line of anointed ones or prophets sent to Israel by Yehovah. Yeshua performed many miracles. So did Moshe. So did Eliyahu, the forerunner of Messiah who announces the coming Great Day of Adonai. We might decide on balance that Moshe's miracles were more spectacular. John the Baptist had a much larger following of people than did Yeshua. Yeshua taught that the people must follow the instructions in Torah. So did Yochanan (John) and Moshe. Yeshua taught that the ancient rabbis should teach *Torat Moshe* rather than their rabbinic oral traditions of men. Yeshua pointed his people away from the religious slavery of ancient rabbinic Judaism and back to Torah. Moshe led his people away from Egyptian slavery and toward Torah at Mount Sinai. Scriptures say that when Messiah comes there will be peace on earth. Surely Jesus was an anointed prophet who gave his life as a

---

[97] *Ezekial 37 and there are many other examples.*

suffering servant of the Almighty. He neither claimed to be Messiah nor God. Recall that feeling when you learned that there is no Santa Claus? What else has been left out of the NT?

I have found it not good to engage in substantive conversations with Christians unless they demonstrate early that they are open to Semitic roots truths. Otherwise their resulting one sided arguments are pointless. I have already heard all their tortured rationales and for 50+ years. I stupidly made them myself, before realizing I was off Yehovah's narrow trail. And, too much drama for me. I can understand a person who perceives that he has done the right thing and therefore all other positions deserve a strong reaction. However I believe that if one takes hold of the most ancient words of Yehovah, in context, and ignores all subsequent human massaging of them, then any reasonable person should be able to appreciate that Torah is the overlooked alternative deserving some real attention. **God Hates Religion** says if you built your foundation on the sand of the Greek and Latin derived King James scriptures emphasizing the NT, you need to go back another 2,000 years to authentic Hebrew and Aramaic Scriptural bedrock. You need to Seek the Ancient Ways of Yehovah.

If you have lots of Christian experience, you have been taught to worship Jesus, somehow, as God. And it is a fact that nowhere even in your own NT scriptures does Jesus claim to be Savior nor God. When Yeshua is quoted in the first person, he is talking as the living Torah and mouthpiece of Yehovah. He is not referring personally to himself. To accept this fact, you do not have to give up your intimate spiritual relationship with the Almighty. You probably already half recognize that it is Yehovah and Him alone who is God Almighty and that you should worship Him, not any part of creation. When Pontius Pilate asked Yeshua whether he was the Messiah (Are you the King of the Jews?) Jesus reportedly replied: "You say that I am." Meaning *he*, Jesus, had never claimed to be the great **I am** (Yehovah). This is a pun.

Is there a place in NT scriptures where Yeshua specifically claims to be Messiah? GHR could not find it. The concept of Messiah is not even identified in the most revered scroll of Isaiah, but Messianic functions are described there. Yeshua was accorded, by default, the status of kosher Rabbi. Consider this episode in his life:

Yeshua traveled from synagogue to synagogue and with him went the people. Large crowds followed him, which meant they left their home synagogue. So, one synagogue is jammed with people while all the nearby synagogues are empty. Empty as in no offering money. How do you suppose the rabbis at each of those empty synagogues felt about Jesus' travels? (He was brought before Pontius Pilate eventually because he was interfering with these ancient rabbis' livelihoods. But the criminal charge was analogous to rebel terrorism.) Because of the large number of the people in attendance at any given synagogue, and all following Yeshua, he was given the honor of reading Torah. It is recorded at Luke 4, 18 to 21 that Yeshua was handed the scroll of the prophet Isaiah and he found the place where it is written and read aloud saying:

"The Spirit of Adonai is upon me; Therefore he has anointed me to announce Good News to the poor; he has sent me to proclaim freedom for the imprisoned and renewed sight for the blind, to release those who have been crushed, to proclaim a year of the favor of Adonai." [98]

This above quote from Luke is a quote from Isaiah 61 reproduced below:

"The Spirit of Adonai Elohim is upon me, because Adonai has anointed me to announce good news to the poor. He has sent me to heal the brokenhearted; to proclaim freedom to the captive, to let out into light those bound in the dark; to proclaim the year of the favor of Adonai." [99]

After closing the scroll and returning it to the *Shammash*, he sat down; and the eyes of everyone in the synagogue were fixed upon Yeshua. And, from Luke 4, 21 **CJB** Yeshua said:

"Today, as you heard it read, this passage of the Tanakh was fulfilled!"

Why were the eyes of all fixed on Him? Because they recognized that he had not read to them the entire Scriptural reading for that day. They knew what it should have said, they had heard it for years. These people were all crammed into the synagogue in hopes of finally hearing Yeshua reveal to them that he was indeed Messiah. But he stopped short of the full reading, he left out the most important part of Isaiah 61. What he did read is that he was anointed to be Adonai's servant, to heal and to *announce* good tidings of good things to come (The Good News). What he left out is the beautiful part where Jesus recites that he is here *now* as Messiah to make everything right in the world. He did not say the last half of the verse: " *and the day of vengeance of our God; to comfort all that mourn;* "[100] He also did not say the verses which followed and describe Messiah's other functions. He stopped right before the day of vengeance. Why? The *day of vengeance of our God* refers to a function attributed to Messiah in other Tanakh Scriptures where Messiah disarms the nations of the earth and clears the way for Yehovah's rule in righteousness over the whole earth by

---

[98] *Luke 4, 18 and 19. Complete Jewish Bible*
[99] *Isaiah 61, 1 and 2a. Complete Jewish Bible*
[100] *New King James Version*

Torah. Yeshua read only the first part which portrays his role as the Anointed One or Suffering Servant. Then, he proclaimed "this day" that he as a prophet was fulfilling that first "announcing" part of the prophecy in their hearing. This is an instance when he purposefully avoided claiming himself to be The Messiah. Either that or Luke's report of this event is factually incorrect. Take your choice. Finally, if one looks at Luke 4, verse 24, Yeshua again specifically aligns himself with all the prophets of old.

Elsewhere Yeshua refers to himself as also the fulfillment of Torah in the flesh. **[Think not that I have come to destroy Torah, I have not come to destroy, but to fulfill Torah...].** Here destroy means change. He died as the fulfillment of Torah in the flesh. Did he die to save you from your sins? That interpretation destroys Torah words. You are only a sinner as long as you choose to not observe Torah lifestyle. We cannot have another Savior in addition to Yehovah, we need to observe Torah. Yehovah alone is our only Savior (stated in Isaiah 43, 11 *et.al.*). Too simple for you? Remember that it all has to be simple enough for a 8 year old to understand. Since virtually all Christian teachings flow from foreign translations of Hebrew scriptures, no Christian is likely to ever realize on their own that they have been worshiping a kosher rabbi as God. How could you possibly know therefore that his ministry and death were all about defending Moshe's written Torah against the human traditions of the ancient rabbi's oral traditions. This is a clear function of Yehovah's prophets. An example of this assertion is the episode reported where Yeshua threw out the ancient rabbi's moneychangers from the temple saying: [*"My father's house is a house of prayer, but you have made it a den of robbers"*]. Moshe's written Torah described the Jerusalem Temple as Yehovah's Sanctuary, a house of prayer; Torah is the Great Equalizer. There is Yehovah way up there and then there is all of us humans, even the priests, all on the same level. The ancient Temple rabbis developed traditions in which they became a ruling class of Temple aristocracy allowing them to function far beyond the Torah boundaries of Temple offering procedures. They should have been the servants of the people, but they went into business for themselves in the temple treasury. They were in effect financially exploiting the temple and preying upon the people. So:

"I am going to bring disaster on this people; it is the consequence of their own way of thinking; for they pay no attention to my words; and as for my Torah, they reject it." [101]

"It is the consequence of their own way of thinking" and **"...they pay no attention to my words..."** are interpreted, with respect to the theme of this book, as

---

[101] *Jeremiah 6, 16; and 19b and 20.*

applying to any who have accepted someone else's rules for living, another human's designation of what is holy and over time becoming *their* traditions all woven into a new religion. Masterful. The Holy One of Israel has mapped out for us in Torah the ancient Way to worship Him. The proof is the longevity of His witnesses, the nation of Israel. The passages also *prophetically* refer to discarding His Words and *reconstructing* the Aramaic and Hebrew writings of the NT to create a new set of holy traditions: Such as calling Jesus both God and Messiah, then calling both God and Jesus by the term Lord. This is the heart of the Torah Changed foundation of Gospel teachings. Anyone who does this has unwittingly admitted themselves to a new class of "*This people*" who are on the wrong side of Yehovah's Words, His Torah. He spoke of this many times. This substitution was operational by the end of the first 80 years after the passing of Jesus from this earth. Changes continue to the present days. Jeremiah 6, 16 says rest for one's soul is found by seeking the ancient pathways where the good Way is. Jeremiah lived some 600 years before Jesus. In order for Yehovah's path of the Good Way to be ANCIENT it would have to exist before the time of Yeshua and even before Jeremiah. In contrast, Christian teachings are anachronisms, the timing of cause and effect are reversed. Because of the actual chronology, *it is not written* in Torah Scriptures that your allegiance to Gospel places Judeo Christian you walking on the ancient path where is the Good Way. You are off by at least 2600 years.

    From Yeshua's final act of compassion we know that the practice of a religion is not needed for one to find paradise or rest for one's soul. The "observant" thief on the cross who requested mercy was told that he would be in paradise (a place of rest for his soul) that day. *That day* was the day the thief died: he had no possibility, other than his speech honoring Torah, via Yeshua, of ever participating in any religious act. So by a Jesus event recorded in ☦'s own NT scriptures, Yeshua's words argues against its various teachings of absolute salvation requirements.

Summary

"Seek the Ancient Paths, Where the Good Way Is..."

If you happen to be browsing this summary before reading the book, some cautions. *First*, the English word meanings that you would apply to certain biblical terms presented in this book are not what these terms signified when they were Spoken and written in the ancient Hebrew Scriptures, 3500 years ago. This is of major importance because the Author of these terms, the Creator of the universe, El, Adonai, Eloheinu HaShem Yehovah cast them in concrete with: **Do Not Change My Words**. And we show you many words in modern English bibles which do not at all convey the original significance of the ancient biblical words. The effect of changing His Words is that His Ways, His plans for us are not communicated, lost. *Secondly*, you are being asked to take in 35 years of the author's gradually consolidated Torah discoveries in the short time period spent reading this book, a few days, more or less. To adjust for that reality may require additional readings. This book is my written report of many years of tiny steps I have taken. A long process begun by refusing to continue glossing over inconsistencies between the bible's words and church teachings. In the end, these 35 years later, my unavoidable conclusion is that too many church descriptions of God's Ways radically differ from their original characterizations by Yehovah. And this is in the church's own Scriptural foundation: the Hebrew bible, or Torah. Torah contains the oldest events of the bible and the written down Sayings of the Creator.

If you jump into this book insisting upon the meanings of today's English Bible's words, expect a negative book experience and continued ignorance of the Almighty's Ways. While Torah teaches Yehovah's Ways, which are His ancient plans for humanity, religions teach human theories of God: theologies. The words of Torah display the singular intelligence in the Almighty's Ways with critical information that is missing in modern English bibles and church teachings. Yehovah's Words literally describe Himself: "......*My Ways are higher than your ways and My thoughts are higher than your thoughts....* ", so DO NOT CHANGE MY WORDS.

This researcher took an intellectual sabbatical from his familial religion a few years before 2005 at which time he began acquainting himself with Torah using this *Scripture noir* approach to its word meanings: What did the words mean back then at the time they were spoken? This approach allows us to go around all disconnected modern religious behaviors and semantics and back to the thinking of Yehovah. There were many exciting discoveries over the last ten years. Here are a few: Yehovah and Moses had quite a few face to face discussions during the forty years after Mt. Sinai and for this he stands out from all other post Adam human beings. One face to face involved impossible challenges Israel experienced keeping a Torah provision. The Almighty advised Moses of an acceptable solution (e.g. one time, Yehovah accepted the chief priest's (Hezekiah's) prayer for forgiveness for the entire nation :); A persistent theme throughout Torah is mercy for the helpless and disadvantaged; Often Torah accounts of various events are not chronological, take care; The Messianic believers; Torah keeping Christians; The Hebrew perspective of the bible; The Berean church, Jewish heroes whose dedication to their Torah standard is only briefly mentioned in the NT; Foreign writings altered the Semitically written NT to create a new religion for gentiles around a new creation known as The Gospel; Many Christian traditions are from pagan sources; Shaul (Paul) was a counterfeit follower of God's Anointed One, Jesus, and was active creating a new religion only after Jesus left this earth; Paul wrote a large proportion of what became a new bible for gentiles, but he rarely even quotes Jesus casting some measure of doubt upon its historical accuracy; Jesus did not write *anything* in it; The NT provides no statement by Yeshua personally claiming to be Messiah, nor God: WHAT!!; There is no NT record of any face to face discussions between Jesus and Yehovah; After Jesus' passing, the teachings and activities of the leader of all Jesus' disciples was James, Jesus' stepbrother; Peter, Paul and John reported to James at his HQ in Jerusalem; James' leadership activities over Jesus disciples is almost completely omitted from the **Acts** of the Jewish Apostles; New theological teachings in Paul's religious writings in the years after the passing of Jesus, in contrast, are covered in great detail throughout the NT; In these, Paul entirely omits Jesus' relentless teaching for the house of Israel to return to Moses' Torah; Mistranslated wordings throughout the NT obscure the Torah basis of all Jesus' teachings; Paul did not reproduce Jesus' teachings, but recast them into gospel theologies; Understanding Torah is not presently a sure thing as some ancient Hebrew words are uncommon or are used in uncommon ways, or have multiple meanings; When one is confronted with Hebraic words of uncertain meaning, valid commentary can be found by consulting expert Hebrews who live the Hebraic perspective handed down through the generations by the righteous keepers of ancient Torah: such as this book's Torah experts.

The personal [102] *Presence* of the Almighty was revealed on planet earth at Mt. Sinai some 3500 years ago. Yehovah dwelled on His land with His people, Israel. This book describes the import of that Event and also historical episodes relating to His Presence here on earth. These events took place east of the Mediterranean Sea in a geographical area known as the southern levant, ten time zones around the world from western North America. Down through the ages, generations of foreigners have manipulated the details and impact of that Event for their own advantage. Now these millennia later, few people truly grasp the overpowering fact of Yehovah's Presence here on earth. This loss of focus marginalizes not only the Almighty's Presence in *eretz Israel*, but also the teachings in His Speeches to the nation of Israel

At the time of Yehovah's arrival in the Middle East, life in America was dominated by *numerous* clans and tribes of Native Americans, tall trees, squirrels, buffalo, deer and huge flocks of passenger pigeons. No antiquities have been found in North America that connect to any event in the Holy Land. Thus an American perspective is not helpful in determining the role of the ancient events in the land of Israel. However, what if some of America's First Generation native Indians are found to be genetically descended from the man Israel? For now and without resorting to speculation, only the tribes making up the nation of Israel have detailed written lineage going back generations before their Abrahamic ancestors to the time of Adam. Jews personally witnessed the Presence of the Creator on *eretz Israel* long ago.

Human beings throughout all time demonstrate a tendency to use shortcuts to achieve control. For foreign religions descended from Torah, religious traditions are man's institutionalized shortcuts to avoid compliance with the unchangeable terms of the Creator's Torah. Where human shortcuts alter Yehovah's Torah Words and pass them off on other people, He Hates It. It means those other people will not know His Ways and consequently be unable to follow Yehovah's doctrine in their daily lifestyles.

God gave speeches to the descendants of the man Israel. In the western world no one cares. In the record of the Almighty's oldest recorded Sayings, Torah, 𐤉𐤄𐤅𐤄 spoke His vision for human life on earth. It was a one time event and it was

---

[102] *Moses was allowed to see Yahweh's "back" as He passed by and on many occasions spoke face to face with Him, not true of any other person, ever!*

documented in Hebrew Scriptures. Through the ages various individual humans accumulated political power and constructed religious traditions that they themselves declared to be HOLY. It continues throughout the world today. **God Hates Religion** is not interested in what men have made holy, but reports to you that holiness *springs* only from the Almighty's own Words. Religious translations of Yehovah's Words use anachronisms, contextual deprivations and tricks to construct alternative standpoints with which to alter translations of the Almighty's Words. You found in this book evidence that by Yehovah's design only His Torah has endured unchanged. So:

We gentiles have all been misled by our forefathers.

For many reasons human beings for hundreds of generations have disrespected Adonai Elohim Yehovah. Casting aside His Words, humans have greatly diverged in their misunderstanding of His ancient Writings in Hebrew and Aramaic. Divergent renditions of Torah over time have developed into religions, each claiming to be the one true "way" to God. God did not Speak to Israel in order to promote named religions. No? What about Judaism? This book is practical and, I hope, minimally academic. **God Hates Religion is written to gentile ignorance of Torah**. What Yehovah does with His servant Israel and their keeping of Torah is His Business. However, God's Sayings *are* shown here to denigrate foreign religions, especially when they operate on His land. His speeches are for us the important part of His interactions with human history. When the two stone tablets and the Ark of the Covenant are revealed for the world to experience, all will appreciate its beauty and realize the cumulative impact of its words for each of us. At that time this book's conclusions not presently accepted by Christians should be realized as remarkably biblical.

The events chronicling the history of the nation of Israel have been communicated to us through Semitic writings some of which approach 4,000 years of age. The Tanakh documents the events of this history in Hebrew and Aramaic. Similarly, the NT's words, originally written down in Aramaic, detail holy land events which were spoken in the Aramaic language. Both Hebrew and Aramaic use the same 22 pictographic derived symbols to represent spoken consonant sounds. Hebrew words consist of three consonants written down without vowels. Archaeological evidence shows that Canaanite laborers traveled from the land of Canaan to Egypt to work in turquoise mines during the reign of Pharaoh Amenemhet III (1853 to 1803 B.C.E.).

They wrote graffiti on their work site cave walls in paleo pictographs[103] using an unpolished but elegant Semitic aleph beit of only 22 symbols. This is in contrast to the thousands of symbols in Egyptian hieroglyphics. Yehovah was scribed with this symbol, but 10x oversized: ᗡ. Three hundred years after this graffiti, Torah was scribed in these paleo Hebrew pictographic symbols and in these symbols the Ten Commandments and Yehovah's other Sayings, instructions, and statutes were written down. Here's the rub: while the lead character in Torah is Yehovah, the NT has two stars: *Y'shua* (Jesus) in the first part whose sayings are connected to Torah, due to his quotes of it. The second is *Shaul* (Paul), Y'shua's chief persecutor whose later teachings of new theories replaced Yeshua's teachings of Torah. Shaul's foreign language abstractions created a new religion with a new bible and new man made ideas of what humans should call holy.

Comprehensive historical accounts of first century events comes from a collection of writings in Aramaic by a Jewish historian named *Josephus*. Josephus, a Jew, wrote to a Roman audience, hence his Roman name. There are also numerous foreign translations of the Aramaic NT, numerous historical writings not canonized into biblical Scriptures and thousands of detailed clay tile foreign records going back more than four thousand years. There are also the ongoing findings of Hebraic archaeology in and near the holy land. There is the Hebrew semantic knowledge of modern Messianic teachers such as Michael Rood, Jonathon Bernis and Sid Roth. There is the ancient Hebrew linguist, Nehemiah Gordon and biblical archaeologists such as Dr. James D. Tabor, Simca Jacobovici and Dr. Orly Goldwasser. **God Hates Religion** drew on all these sources plus others for its characterization of a Jewish perspective. The NT begins with five historical books spoken and written by Israelites for the benefit of Israelites all in the Aramaic language. Yeshua and his talmadim all spoke Aramaic in the Galilean dialect.[104] Early Galileans, living in the land of Canaan before the nation of Israel arrived brought this speech back with them from Babylon. They crossed back into Palestine over the Euphrates river before Moshe's time and millennia before Yeshua. The NT was written expressly to Jews in the historical context of Jewish details of Temple rituals, feast days, holy days and other Jewish ordinances of Torah. Translations and rewrites of these Aramaic NT documents deleted most Jewish details

---

[103] *Proto Sinaitic pictograms for Hebrew word sounds could have adapted from hieroglyphics as private "codes" developed by laborers while indentured either in Serabit el Khadem, Egypt or hundreds of years earlier from Joseph during his 13 year Egyptian imprisonment. Captive people develop and modify symbols as secret codes. Witness the modified Morse code created and used by American POWs various wars of the 20th century. Moses could have been a source also.*
[104] *Mark 14, 70.*

altering the context. Missing is information about the Torah keeping activities of Yeshua's followers who continued to observe Yeshua's Torah lifestyle after his passing. Individual Christians nowadays are relatively ignorant of the true circumstances represented by NT passages in their bibles, because the Jewish context is minimized. In George Lamsa's Aramaic translation of the NT, many phrases have a note explaining Aramaic idioms which have for centuries misled English readers of western bibles. These surprises are the tip of the iceberg. The NT writings used as a bible by Christians are not the Scriptures referred to throughout the NT nor by Yeshua. The NT had not been written yet. The NT is post Biblical, written after Torah. Any quotations of Scripture in the NT all refer to the Hebrew Torah (Tanakh). That was their bible. It was Yeshua's bible. Yeshua was Torah observant. If you name the name of Jesus, but are not Torah observant, then you have failed to follow his example. Are you greater than your Master? The NT stories and teachings have been presented to you incomplete, out of context and with anachronisms as "proofs" of Christian traditional teachings. **Any of the church's spiritual laws which differ from Tanakh teachings are made up.** You should realize that this has caused you to follow another religion and in fact "another Jesus", a Greek Jesus stripped of his Torah mission and Torah lifestyle. Jesus did not promote abstractions such as gospel and he avoided gentiles.

Modern Christian teachings tell us to follow the gospel found in the New Testament (NT) which *supercedes* not only Torah but the entire Old Testament (OT).[105] Yehovah explains (Isaiah 29, 13) that this kind of thinking distances one's heart from Him! Christian traditions claim that their new teachings exempt them from the absolutes of the Torah of the Almighty. No one is. Consider Yehovah's direct expressed promise to the Rechabite clan of Canaanites who were gentiles that He would ensure there will "never cease to be a Rechabite man *standing before Me*", Jeremiah ch. 35, 1 to 19. In this fascinating example, the basis for *deliverance* for a gentile family is their steadfast determination to follow exactly a Kenite family edict from their family patriarch, Jonadab, descendant of their ancient patriarch Jethro who was the Canaanite father in law of Moses! This extraordinary Way of Yehovah is a clue for us that from God's perspective if the Rechabites can remain faithful to a family patriarch's words for generations, so can Israel be faithful to Torah. By extension, if your God is the God of Israel you are accountable to Torah.

Arguably no Christian believes every traditional teaching of their church. And many *individual* Christians remain very curious about the Hebrew roots of their faith,

---

[105] *Yehovah REALLY does not like this. Isaiah 29, 13 CJB.*

knowing that the first half of their bible, Tanakh, was the only authority Jesus quoted for his teachings. **In Isaiah 29, 14 God specifically promises bafflement, disappearing wisdom *and* ruin for those who worship Him by the mitzvah (commandments, plans, thinking, or traditions) of men.** So, this book's title. The challenge for us westerners is to make sure we do not get caught worshiping the Almighty with empty words from our mouths (by the traditions of men) while our hearts are far from His ancient Ways. GHR examined in detail this contrast of the Torah worship of Yehovah versus the "lip service" of human traditions. The Almighty is not happy about new foreign cultural traditions changing His Torah and He has spoken of the consequences.

At this particular time in the human history of planet earth, any of us could make ourselves personally aware of the Ways of Yehovah, the Living God of Israel. To observe Torah, one could "join" the World Karaite Movement or utilize the wealth of Torah information via cyberspace at KaraiteKorner.org, *et.al.*. Yeshua lived and taught a message of **Return to Torah** to his fellow Judeans for the benefit of the ten northern tribes of Israel. Leave your western gentile pagan ways behind in favor of the Sayings of the God of Yeshua and seek to become a sojourner with Israel via Torah observance. Embracing His Torah in terms of its own context provides your personal link to Yehovah. The crucial issue in life is: **Does Yehovah Know You?** If anyone personally observes Torah, He is known by Yehovah. Our personal path to God's Ways is Torah as suggested in Jeremiah 6, 16 which says in the *Complete Jewish Bible*:

"**Stand at the crossroads and look: ask about the ancient paths, 'Which one is the good Way?' Take it and you will find rest for your souls..."**

Anyone who does not *Go Ancient* will default into the camp of those standing against Yehovah as described by the balance of the above Jeremiah quote: **"But they said, 'We will not take it.'"** The ideas of those around us, especially from people overtrained in legends by churches, would be irrelevant except that they cause many not to take the good Way of Torah. Job had the same situation with his religious friends. Yehovah spoke to Job of killing them for their false characterization of His Words. In the narration, Yehovah relented when Job intervened to have their lives spared. You could simplify your life, reduce fear, anxiety and guilt and realize the beauty of Yehovah's thinking in your life, simply by acknowledging His Words in their context, no matter what. We all need help understanding His Torah. GHR suggests Nehemia Gordon and *some* modern Karaites for this role.

By his own NT recorded words, rabbi Yeshua ben Yosef was dedicated to returning the lost house of Israel to Yehovah's written Torah of Moshe. He mentioned the land *eretz Israel*, not the entire planet. He did mention fulfilling Torah and

Prophecy. Christian churches do not teach these facts nor their implications. You, individual Christian could live out your life centered upon Yehovah and following Jesus' Torah teachings in the fullness of their Torah context. Teach that to your children. Yehovah's Speeches to the nation were witnessed by two million descendants of the man Israel at Mount Sinai some 1500 years before rabbi Yeshua's time on earth. Yet within the short time frame of fifty years after Yeshua's passing, Yeshua's Jewish followers, the Yeshuaites, were outnumbered by gentile believers who redefined his teachings to their own foreign terms. Seeking to distance themselves from their Israelite mentors [106] they *spiritualized* Yeshua's teachings into a new gentile friendly religion, using Greek translations to accomplish the alterations. This expunged original Torah terms and Judaic details of the Yeshuaites from new Greek translations of NT.

How can we reconcile the fact that Yeshuaite Torah observant practices at the Jerusalem headquarters **were sufficient to result in the receiving of the Ruach Ha Kodesh (Holy Spirit), but not sufficient for inclusion in the NT??** Whoever was responsible for this scriptural crime poked a finger in God's eye. As the new gentile religion emerged, priestly duties were taken over by gentile clergy and a name for *it* was taken from a foreign polytheistic concept (christos). As an accumulated result of these changes to the Torah teachings of the Jesus and his Yeshuaites, the World Christian Encyclopedia reported that by the year 2,000 C.E. 34,800 denominations of the Christian religion had been observed world wide. It adds that their only common thread is that there is no common thread. GHR can suggest one: Shaul's Gospel, substituting human spiritual constructs for Yehovah's simple concrete Torah words.

As noted in the Glossary chapter, modern church teachings include pagan names, terms, concepts and legendary traditions from the worship of pagan gods of ancient middle eastern foreign countries and nearby regions. Yehovah said many times in Torah not to worship Him in pagan ways, nor make any additions or subtractions to Torah. Yet churches continue to claim our NT replaces Yehovah's Torah. **The term Judeo Christian is an oxymoron** for all who are trapped by Christianity's pagan teachings which do not reproduce Jesus' Torah life. But, **Torah observant Christians who live and worship Yehovah as Yeshua did, truly live as Judeo Christians.**

Graciousness is a personality characteristic of Yehovah activated when He perceives someone He likes. It's how He feels when He says, "Look! It's my servant Job. Now there's a servant." And, if joy is not what Yehovah feels, grace is missing from the relationship: He considers someone, but His Eyes are not warm. The Hebrews are God's best and oldest friends, what chance would a gentile Torah repudiator have to

---

[106] *For their military attempts to reestablish Torah observance in the land of Israel, Rome considered the " mentors", rabbis actually, to be anarchists, i.e. terrorists..*

cause Yehovah's eyes to twinkle with joy? Expect consequences. For example in Ezekial's vision in chapters 8 through 11, Yehovah killed all the men, Jew and gentile alike who were in Jerusalem and found to not be actively lamenting the practice of pagan religions by others in that city of **Yehovah's refuge**. What a thing! To be killed by God! All those who lamented paganisms in Jerusalem received a mark on their forehead which signified that Torah dwelled in their hearts, the Almighty's grace in action. Our Christian churches teach that a forehead mark will in the future be a bad sign. See how man's ideas adjust Torah for a new outcome? Now that you have read this book, issues such as the forehead marks should provide you with the basis to reconsider for yourself whose doctrine will reside in your heart. We need Revelation reconciled to Ezekial and NT to Torah. *Some Day* men from all nations will pilgrimage to Jerusalem for Hebraic teaching:[107] to know and understand Yehovah.[108] Meanwhile, Jerusalem remains filled with foreign religions ignoring Torah and practicing paganisms on His sanctuary ground.

A Christian sentiment I have heard is: "I don't care what you say. I have a personal relationship with Jesus. I have Jesus in my heart and nothing you can say is going to change that." This common misconception is predicted by none other than Jesus: *"You err, not knowing the Scriptures"*; And, *"Keep away from me O you who work iniquity."* Recall that the word iniquity refers to living a ***Torahless*** life. Sooo, Torah keepers (righteous) should not allow Torah breakers (pagans) to judge them.

Christians and Messianics identify Yeshua ben Yosef haMashiach as the Son of God. Yet NT scriptures do not quote Yeshua as claiming that for himself. Instead he calls himself "son of man" thus arraying himself with an ancient procession of chosen anointed ones (prophets, kings) of Yehovah. **OTHER PEOPLE** called him the Son of God. Do not be unwittingly led by other people's pagan gods. In Yeshua's teachings he spoke as the mouthpiece of Yehovah's Torah, Torah in the flesh, in his heart. Anyone who elevates rabbi Yeshua to the level of the Almighty worships a created being, not the Almighty. Read the nineteen Scriptures below and you will find described to you in the words of the Almighty: what His Name is; Why worshiping anyone or anything else is an abomination to Yehovah; Why human thinking which seeks a way around Torah is useless; And finally why we conclude that He hates religion. After setting aside our religion, these Scriptures were very good to read aloud in our "tent" on Sabbath eve:

☞ ***Deuteronomy*** *32, 1 through 4: My words describe how I am.*

Revelation *15, 3 and 4: Songs of Moshe and Lamb sung in praise of Yehovah.*

---

[107] *Zechariah 8, 23.*
[108] *Revelation 15, 4.*

Deuteronomy 6, 4 to 9: The Sh'mah. Recited three times daily by Yeshua.

Jeremiah 12, 1: Why does the way of the wicked prosper? Answer in 12, 2B: You Yehovah are near in their mouths (words) but far from their hearts.

Jeremiah 9, 23 and 24: [**Men glory in their wisdom, might and wealth. Glory in this: that you understand and know Me.**] Recall Ezekial 8 through 11.

Jeremiah 6, 19 and 20: [**In vain people worship Me , preferring their own man made rules to My Torah. I will bring disaster upon them.**] Recall Ezekial 8 through 11.

Jeremiah 6, 16: [**Stand in the ways look, ask for the old ways where the good way is and if you walk in it you will find rest for your souls**].

Zechariah 1 and Malachi 3: **I am jealous for Yerusalayim** (Yehovah's sanctuary city) **and Tziyon** (the nation of Israel).

Isaiah 42, 8 and 43, 10: [**I am Yehovah, that is My Name. I share my glory with NO ONE ELSE, nor do I yield my praise to any idol**] ; and [**You Israel are my witnesses that no god existed before Me nor was any god created after me. I alone am Yehovah**]. So we have to go to His witnesses to find our way back to Him.

Exodus 6, 2 and 3: *[God said to Moshe:* **I am yod hei vav hei, Yehovah***]*.

Deuteronomy 10, 12: *follow My ways, obey My Torah....*

Genesis 12, 3: Yehovah's covenant with Abraham and his descendants: "I will bless those who bless you, but I will curse anyone who curses you; and by you all the families of the earth will be blessed......." *Complete Jewish Bible.*

Isaiah 63, 8 and 9; Yehovah became their Savior and in all their troubles, He was troubled. Then the Messenger of His face saved them.

Isaiah 43, 11: "I, even I am Yehovah and besides Me there is no Savior".

Isaiah 44, 6: " Thus says Adonai, Israel's King and Redeemer, Adonai Tzva'ot: I am the first and I am the last; besides me there is no god."*Complete Jewish Bible.*

Numbers 6, 22 to 27: The Aaronic prayer: [**Adonai said to Moshe: give this prayer to Aharon and sons. With it you shall bless the people of Israel.**]; Note, gentile Sojourners are also the people of Israel.

Deuteronomy 32, 39 and 43: "Now see that I, even I, am He, And there is no God besides Me. I kill and I make alive; I wound and I heal; Nor is there any who can deliver from My hand". And more hope for gentile sojourners: "**Rejoice O Gentiles, with His people; For He will avenge the blood of His servants**".

While all of us wish for an end to heartache, mourning, war and death, too few at the present time seriously consider the *coming day* when Yehovah makes good on his Words and rules the earth by Torah in righteousness, justice and peace; A time when He rewards believers who know and understand Him. Too few seriously take a *no matter what attitude*, sell themselves out to Yehovah and adopt the Torah lifestyle of Jesus in order to know and understand Yehovah. Meanwhile, all of creation awaits the return of Yehovah to His Sanctuary land, *eretz Israel*.

The seeds of modern Christian beliefs were borrowed from middle eastern pagans lurking in the days of prehistory and ancient Scriptural events. The incorporation of pagan practices by Christianity (see chapter 3) resulted in its 34,800+ distinct movements. Religions deflect God seekers away from the Torah lifestyle God intended for all of humanity.[109] Yehovah hates the existence of foreign gods in His Sanctuary, the Land He set aside for Himself as His inheritance, *Eretz Israel*. He hates being worshiped in ways borrowed from the worship of pagan gods. So, the title of this book.[110] *One Day* gentiles will come from all over the world to learn about Yehovah. They are prophesied to request of a Jewish rabbi, teach us Yehovah's Ways for: **"Our fathers have inherited lies, worthless and unprofitable things."** [111] *Some Day* these ancient words first used on Pharoah may be heard again, but this time put to the world's religions: *Let my people go. Let all my people, including the sons of My gentile Sojourners, go. I Am Yehovah.*

Any individual Christian now knows the way to be both follower of Jesus *and* observer of Yehovah's Torah. Some astute ministers are already taking into account members of their congregation seeking Jewish roots. *Some Day w*hen there are enough of us, Christian churches will have no need to teach anything. Becoming a Torah observant or *enabled* Christian takes heart, freely available from a steadfast Yehovah. Many readers will not be able throw off centuries of lies from our forefathers just from a first look at this book. However, books last a long time....

Until there is some size to the present remnant of sojourner Yeshuaites, *fellowship* may be limited to family: the biblical definition of *gathering*. Live by trust; Trust in Yehovah's Words. Torah teaches us to come together on Shabbat with our own family in our "tent" and remain at home from sundown to sundown on Shabbat. **We can take heart as we gather our family at the appointed times, knowing we are synchronized by His calendar, all of us worldwide observing his ancient Ways together.** Biblically, fellowship happens at home.

The braver among us may forge Torah ahead in individual churches but are cautioned not to find themselves creating a new religion. The future is Yehovah's.

---

[109] *Matthew 15, 8 and 9, meaning the teachings of men replace Torah in the peoples' hearts.*
[110] *Ezekial chapters 8 through 11.*
[111] *Jeremiah 16, 18 and 19.*

Appendix

This old introduction ended up on the cutting room floor. It has details recounting how this book came about and is shown here for the record. JMR

This author left his lifelong Christian faith behind for seven years and single mindedly followed the trail back to the ancient Words of the Almighty in search of their pristine significance. The challenge was to find the bona fide meanings of the Words of the Hebrew's God in relation to the circumstances of their writing with no religious filtering. Fortunately much relevant information is available in English. The search led to the doorsteps of certain Torah observant Hebrews whom this researcher found standing as both the living witnesses and the context of the Almighty's ancient Words (Torah). Along the journey there were many surprises and they grouped around the fact that the God of Abraham and Yeshua just doesn't like man made religions. There were many surprises, e.g. pagan beliefs are firmly incorporated in Christian traditions; Secondly the New Testament is missing in its report of first century history most of the teachings and actions of the Jerusalem church and its leader during the 40 years between Jesus' death and the destruction of Jerusalem: a vacant gap; This book reports the Almighty's graphic Words to the Hebrews, but is not a book about Judaism: it's a book about His Words. All Christians are urged to seek the original Hebraic perspective of Scriptures and consider them not as an adjunct to Christian teachings, but **the original doctrine** of Yehovah lived by Yeshua; Later, new, gentile Christian traditions replaced Yehovah's ancient Sayings, going far beyond the Torah that Yeshua lived and taught. I challenge you to open your mind to the intelligence to be found in Yehovah's Words spoken to Moshe in the Torah Scriptures that Yeshua believed to be the bible.

It came to me three or four decades ago that God had condemned public praying more than two thousand years ago. However, praying in front of others is alive and thriving in modern churches. I lived with that, despising outloud prayers, and over the years tried to at least minimize *my* praying outloud. Eventually I centered on the public prayer veto in scriptures boldly written in red type where Jesus says to do it in private. Even adjusting for literary hyperbole, this still puts prayer in a closet, total privacy. In Matthew 6, 1 to 18 Yeshua tells his followers not to give to the poor, nor fast, nor pray in the presence of men. Yeshua ordered his followers to ONLY pray in privacy[112]. In this clear statement, Yeshua was merely expanding on a point from his bible: the Tanakh. He was not making a new law. In Tanakh, the reason given for the prohibition against public religious acts was conceited motivation. Public exhibitions while mourning the

---

[112] Matthew 6,6.

dead are also forbidden because they are also done **to be seen by men.** The bible does not prohibit tattoos. The prohibition against tattoos occurs only in the **context** of mourning the dead. Context literally means " with the text". There is no general prohibition against tatoos.

The book you are peeking at is written to anyone who is troubled by church traditions inconsistent with biblical foundation such as the universally violated prayer veto above. For myself, to truly seek to know and understand the God of Jeremiah, I found it necessary to track down and personally adopt His Words even though it involved relinquishing the ancestral family religion. If it comes to you to give up your religion and live by His Words alone, trust in Yehovah and faith in the original meaning of His Words becomes a real life issue. That is exactly what motivated me to spend 7 years researching my way through the Hebraic roots of Scriptures (*and another 2+ writing this book, ed.:*). From the beginning I did not read Hebrew or Paleo Hebrew and so sources were limited to what is available in English. You could hack your way through the 23 books listed in the Bibliography or find your own sources. Or you could more quickly make your way through the 17 codependent parts of this book. Quickly does not mean easily. We humans tend toward ourselves, but the Almighty reveals what pleases Him is when we pursue **knowing** and **understanding** Him. Any other goal is either peripheral or a diversion created for human convenience, grating on Yehovah.

Other personal shortcuts to status in churches arise from people blindly following church traditions. Here are two that we see elsewhere in the book as examples of what causes the Almighty to turn His Face away. Really not much has changed from Yeshua's nixing these tweaks of religious acts for personal gain. He extensively lists them in Matthew 6, 1 to 18, a section easily overlooked as it is overshadowed by its posting of the Lord's Prayer. Traditional church and its events foster various levels of spoken prayer *competition* or at least social validation. Additionally, in some Protestant churches there is the phenomenon of the Number 2 Guy. He is the wannabe clergyman, a person determined to work his way to PRO. One element of this motivation is having one's own name and life promoted higher. What is higher? Well, God's Name is higher. It's also one aspect of having named Denominations (a Name Game: XYZ Denomination holds itself higher than the others, hence closer to God). Torah functions to place all persons on the same level, even the priests! In western movies the Number 2 Guy's role is similar to that of the "sidekick." He is the church's "prospect" [113] so pastors let him do the praying or fulfill other LEADER roles. Cartoonish characters

---

[113] *For a time I was the local VP of a three patch motorcycle club, where a prospect's life is the opposite of the Number 2 guys'. Earlier I had put in 4 years of meetings every Tuesday night with Oz and Colin Harley Ott to restart the local Christian Motorcyclists Association chapter, then I gave up religion.*

spring to mind from such prospective efforts: Yogi Bear, Howdy Doody, Bat Man's Robin. Sure hope Yehovah appreciates humor.[114] Clergy and Number 2 people everywhere should note that Tanakh Scriptures say Yehovah insists His priests be selected on the sole basis of tribal genetics. God has chosen but human beings promote, especially themselves.

The cumulative weight of unscriptural issues led at last to a personal blow out, a dead end. Church interpretations of Yeshua's teachings are inconsistent even with the theological messages of his biblical quotes from the Tanakh. His quotes show that he was Torah observant. He kept the Sabbath, the feasts of Yehovah and recited the Sh'ma three times a day. Here there is irony: Yeshua spent his entire life's work pointing out the many violations of his bible, the Tanakh, in cultural and religious practice all around him. His clashes were with the human religious traditions of the ancient rabbis of his day; Those traditions violated the written Torah of Moses. Similarly, modern Christian church teachings derive not from Torah but from ascriptural traditions of postbiblical sources. Both scenarios, though many years apart, violate Yeshua's bible. "Holy" church traditions fail to agree with the expressed terms of their Torah foundation.[115]

So a day came when I gave up trying to reconcile evolving Christian teachings with the bible and words of Yeshua, their founder. I dropped all religious [116] practices and friends from my life. "It came to me"[117] that years of religious "training" had not created mental structures adequate to understand the words in Yeshua's bible. So, what good is it? I realized I was ignorant of Yeshua's bible. For about six months, I plowed through what was a total FOG of uncertainty. Then there began a search for what is truly from God, the very best words: no churches, no ministers, no Yogi Bears and no crafty interpretations. Are we to believe that the Almighty does not know what He was talking about in the Tanakh writings? **Surely God has spoken His Mind somewhere in the Bible**. I resolved to only follow the biblical words attributed to the Almighty, in their context, from the earliest Scriptures **no matter what**. I can tell you this: as it stands now (up to the western year 2011) you cannot resolve the differences between church characterizations of God's thinking in a Christian English bible with Yehovah's statements in Yeshua's Tanakh bible. You will only bounce back and forth between being a liar and disrespecting the holiness of what is written in Tanakh. BUT, I found a way, a catalyst that links the English and Semitic languages and provides a way for an

---

[114] *President Bill Clinton brokered peace in the middle east in his Oslo Accord. In Hebrew **OSLO** means toilet seat. All U.S. Presidents sellout Israel to link their name historically, hoping in vain for Middle East peace.*
[115] *Here, the first five books of the bible: Genesis, Exodus, Leviticus, Numbers and Deuteronomy. It also is used generically to refer to the entire Tanakh.*
[116] *Defined as nonTorah thinking about how to relate to the Almighty.*
[117] *This little phrase is a vast improvement over, "The Lord told me."*

English speaker to access the plain meaning of the Semitic scriptures, both Tanakh and NT. For several years during this search, I carried in my mind a number of new, seemingly important facts and notions. I could not identify their relationship. No single link for all the ideas revealed itself. This was very troubling and I continued researching until a solution was found. I doubled back many times over the years. I hope you will approach this book in a similar open, discovery mode. And realize that **God Hates Religion** is intended to decrease the amount of time you might journey alone with no meaningful solution to your issues with religion.

One day in 2005 the last of my long held religious beliefs evaporated. I was personally finished with organized religion. All religious and many cultural underpinnings disappeared. My spiritual mind zeroized. Another day, mindlessly channel surfing the television, Pat Robertson's show appeared. The guest was a person with a very unusual demeanor for a pastor. I stopped and watched, trying to figure out what he was all about. Soon it was suggested they end with prayer. The guest's prayer was like lightning from heaven. I loved the grand terms the guest used to describe the Almighty. In total contrast Pat Robertson's prayer immediately brought me back down to the realities of my religious dilemma. The guest's name was Sid Roth. The next day I ordered his book *The Race to Save the World*. It changed my life. Smelling *truth* at last, a few Messianic sources were quickly assembled. Perhaps they would be more "authentic"? It came to me to create a script for an inhome family Sabbath service. The goal was to somehow to honor the Almighty but without the "benefit" of input from human beings: just the family, in our home, no professional holy persons, no bogus translations. A number of attempts somehow circled back to religious tenets. It came to me again to only use His Words and follow them without regard for the outcome. That thought became this book. The exchange of belief for His Words. Constructing a home worship service continued as the Sabbath service script was "improved" by removing elements from various religious persuasions and using only His words in Scriptures. I wrote a letter justifying our home Sabbath ceremony. Soon I began to realize I was trapped and would HAVE to write a book. A short excursion became a decade of work. After most of the research was finished, the ceremony script was replaced to show you one way **God Hates Religion** could be put into practice on the ground. But it smelled like religion. The ceremony script was removed from this book in order not to be "seen of men." My beliefs, my name do not matter; Only the Almighty's Words. No, there is no script .

I was educated to think as a research psychologist and inferential statistician. Then followed interruptions for the military, then corporate life earning money and the later the hard working years, *surviving* with 3 kids. And now at the other end of life, I find I can avoid the fragrance of religion while its is still afar, and know the trail to the Creator of the universe: **Yehovah!**   End of Appendix

Bibliography

1. Roth, Sid. *The Race to Save the World*. Florida: Charisma House, 2004
2. Garr, John D. *Family Sanctuary: Restoring the Biblically Hebraic Home*. Georgia: Restoration Foundation, 2003
3. Kasdan, Barney. *God's Appointed Customs*. Maryland: Lederer books,1996.
4. Bernis, Jonathon. *Messianic Passover* Haggadah. Go to *jewishvoice.com*.
5. Booker, Richard. *Shabbat Shalom*. Texas: Sound of the Trumpet, Inc.,1998
6. Brown, Michael L. *Our Hands are Stained with His Blood*. Pennsylvania: Destiny Images Publishers, Inc. 1992
7. Lancaster, D. Thomas. *Restoration*. Colorado: First Fruits of Zion, Inc. 2005
8. Rood, Michael. *The Pagan-Christian Connections Exposed*. Florida: Bridge Logos, 2004
9. Stern, David H. *Complete Jewish Bible*. Maryland: Jewish NT Publications, Inc. 1998
10. Munk, Rabbi Michael L. *The Wisdom in the Hebrew Alphabet*. New York: Mesorah Publications, Ltd. 2008. (Sixteen conventional printing editions!!)
11. Seekins, Dr Frank T. *Hebrew Word Pictures*. Arizona: Living Word Pictures, Inc. 2003
12. Fox, Everett. *The Five Books of Moses*, New York: Schocken Books, 1997
13. Gordon, Nehemiah. *The Hebrew Yeshua vs. the Greek Jesus*. Hilkiah Press, 2005
14. Gordon, Nehemiah. www.KaraiteKorner.org. Newsletter on Yahoo groups.
15. Gordon, Nehemiah and Johnson, Keith. *A Prayer to Our Father*. Hilkiah Press, 2005
16. *Tanakh: The Holy Scriptures*, New York: Jewish Publication Society, 1985
17. *The Jewish Study Bible*, New York: The Jewish Publication Society, 1999
18. Tabor, James D. *Restoring Abrahamic Faith*. North Carolina: Genesis 2000, 2008
19. Berlin, Adele and Brettler, Marc Zvi, editors. *The Jewish Study Bible*, New York: Oxford University Press, 2004.
20. *Hebrew English Bible*, The Bible Society in Israel, publisher. Jerusalem: 1995.
21. Lewis, Agnes Smith. *Light on the Four Gospels from the Sinai Palimpsest*, Eugene, Oregon: Wipf and Stock. Previously published by Williams and Norgate, London, 1913.
22. Lamsa, George M. *Holy Bible From the Ancient Eastern Text*, New York: Harper Collins, originally published by A.J. Holman Company, 1933.
23. Mahoney, David Daniel. *The Complete Concordance of Torah Commandments*, printed by Lulu.com. Order from *ww.torahcommandments.com ,2009*.
24. Vermes, Geza. "The Jewish Jesus Movement". In *PARTINGS: How Judaism and Christianity Became Two*. Hershel Shanks, Editor. Washington, D.C. Biblical Archaeology Society, 2013.

www.ingramcontent.com/pod-product-compliance
Lightning Source LLC
Chambersburg PA
CBHW070049100426
42734CB00040B/2820